OPPOSING
VIEWPOINTS®
SERIES

D0380617

Rogue Nations

Other Books of Related Interest:

Opposing Viewpoints Series

Democracy

Globalization

Human Rights

India & Pakistan

The Middle East

North & South Korea

Terrorism

Weapons of Mass Destruction

Current Controversies Series

America's Battle Against Terrorism

The Middle East

War

Weapons of Mass Destruction

At Issue Series

Can Democracy Succeed in the Middle East?

Do Nuclear Weapons Pose a Serious Threat?

Is Iran a Threat to Global Security?

Is North Korea a Global Threat?

Nuclear Security

U.S. Policy Toward Rogue Nations

What Is the State of Human Rights?

"Congress shall make
no law . . . abridging
the freedom of speech,
or of the press."

First Amendment to the U.S. Constitution

The basic foundation of our democracy is the First Amendment guarantee of freedom of expression. The Opposing Viewpoints Series is dedicated to the concept of this basic freedom and the idea that it is more important to practice it than to enshrine it.

OPPOSING
VIEWPOINTS®
SERIES

Rogue Nations

Louise Gerdes, Book Editor

GREENHAVEN PRESS

An imprint of Thomson Gale, a part of The Thomson Corporation

THOMSON
━━━★━━━ ™
GALE

Detroit • New York • San Francisco • New Haven, Conn. • Waterville, Maine • London • Munich

THOMSON

GALE

Bonnie Szumski, *Publisher*
Helen Cothran, *Managing Editor*

© 2006 Thomson Gale, a part of The Thomson Corporation.

Thomson and Star Logo are trademarks and Gale and Greenhaven Press are registered trademarks used herein under license.

For more information, contact:
Greenhaven Press
27500 Drake Rd.
Farmington Hills, MI 48331-3535
Or you can visit our Internet site at http://www.gale.com

Cover photographs reproduced by permission of iStockphoto.com (top); iStockphoto.com/ Greg Henry (center); 2006 Jupiterimages Corporation (bottom).

LIBRARY OF CONGRESS CATALOGING-IN-PUBLICATION DATA

Rogue nations / Louise Gerdes, book editor.
    p. cm. -- (Opposing viewpoints)
Includes bibliographical references and index.
    ISBN 0-7377-3421-3 (hardcover lib. : alk. paper) -- ISBN 0-7377-3422-1 (pbk. : alk. paper)
    1. Security, International--Juvenile literature. 2. Terrorism--Juvenile literature. 3. United States--Foreign relations--Juvenile literature. 4. United States--Military policy--Juvenile literature. I. Gerdes, Louise I., 1953– II. Series: Opposing viewpoints series (Unnumbered)
    JZ5588.R64 2007
    355'.033--dc22

                                        2006016737

Printed in the United States of America
10 9 8 7 6 5 4 3 2 1

Contents

Chapter 3: How Do Rogue Nations Threaten Human Rights?

Chapter 4: How Should the Global Community Respond to Rogue Nations?

Why Consider Opposing Viewpoints?

> *"The only way in which a human being can make some approach to knowing the whole of a subject is by hearing what can be said about it by persons of every variety of opinion and studying all modes in which it can be looked at by every character of mind. No wise man ever acquired his wisdom in any mode but this."*
>
> *John Stuart Mill*

In our media-intensive culture it is not difficult to find differing opinions. Thousands of newspapers and magazines and dozens of radio and television talk shows resound with differing points of view. The difficulty lies in deciding which opinion to agree with and which "experts" seem the most credible. The more inundated we become with differing opinions and claims, the more essential it is to hone critical reading and thinking skills to evaluate these ideas. Opposing Viewpoints books address this problem directly by presenting stimulating debates that can be used to enhance and teach these skills. The varied opinions contained in each book examine many different aspects of a single issue. While examining these conveniently edited opposing views, readers can develop critical thinking skills such as the ability to compare and contrast authors' credibility, facts, argumentation styles, use of persuasive techniques, and other stylistic tools. In short, the Opposing Viewpoints Series is an ideal way to attain the higher-level thinking and reading skills so essential in a culture of diverse and contradictory opinions.

In addition to providing a tool for critical thinking, Opposing Viewpoints books challenge readers to question their own strongly held opinions and assumptions. Most people form their opinions on the basis of upbringing, peer pressure, and personal, cultural, or professional bias. By reading carefully balanced opposing views, readers must directly confront new ideas as well as the opinions of those with whom they disagree. This is not to simplistically argue that everyone who reads opposing views will—or should—change his or her opinion. Instead, the series enhances readers' understanding of their own views by encouraging confrontation with opposing ideas. Careful examination of others' views can lead to the readers' understanding of the logical inconsistencies in their own opinions, perspective on why they hold an opinion, and the consideration of the possibility that their opinion requires further evaluation.

Evaluating Other Opinions

To ensure that this type of examination occurs, Opposing Viewpoints books present all types of opinions. Prominent spokespeople on different sides of each issue as well as well-known professionals from many disciplines challenge the reader. An additional goal of the series is to provide a forum for other, less known, or even unpopular viewpoints. The opinion of an ordinary person who has had to make the decision to cut off life support from a terminally ill relative, for example, may be just as valuable and provide just as much insight as a medical ethicist's professional opinion. The editors have two additional purposes in including these less known views. One, the editors encourage readers to respect others' opinions—even when not enhanced by professional credibility. It is only by reading or listening to and objectively evaluating others' ideas that one can determine whether they are worthy of consideration. Two, the inclusion of such viewpoints encourages the important critical thinking skill of objectively evaluating an author's credentials and bias. This evaluation will illuminate an author's reasons for taking a particular stance on an issue and will aid in readers' evaluation of the author's ideas.

It is our hope that these books will give readers a deeper understanding of the issues debated and an appreciation of the complexity of even seemingly simple issues when good and honest people disagree. This awareness is particularly important in a democratic society such as ours in which people enter into public debate to determine the common good. Those with whom one disagrees should not be regarded as enemies but rather as people whose views deserve careful examination and may shed light on one's own.

Thomas Jefferson once said that "difference of opinion leads to inquiry, and inquiry to truth." Jefferson, a broadly educated man, argued that "if a nation expects to be ignorant and free . . . it expects what never was and never will be." As individuals and as a nation, it is imperative that we consider the opinions of others and examine them with skill and discernment. The Opposing Viewpoints Series is intended to help readers achieve this goal.

David L. Bender and Bruno Leone,
Founders

Introduction

> *"American policymakers clearly have adopted the term 'rogue state' into their vocabularies and into their policies. Ironically, while constructing a list of rogue states is not a difficult proposition, determining precisely just what it takes for a state to be considered a rogue is a bit more complex."*
>
> Paul D. Hoyt,
> *political science professor,*
> *West Virginia University*

"Words are important," writes retired colonel Daniel Smith. "They reflect and affect our thoughts by the specific meanings they carry, the concepts they suggest, and the emotions they touch. Their influence on the human psyche, and therefore on our actions, is enormous," he explains. One of the recurrent controversies in the rogue-nation debate is the utility of the rogue-state label. While some believe the term is useful to describe threats to the United States and to global security, others believe it is hypocritical for the United States to label nations as rogues. Still others believe that applying the label to any nation, including the United States, is counterproductive.

The Clinton administration adopted the term "rogue state" in the 1990s to identify nations that it believed posed a threat to world peace. At the time, Clinton deemed Afghanistan, Iran, Iraq, Libya, and North Korea a threat and therefore rogue. Critics of the administration's foreign policy, however, argued that the United States was applying the term unfairly. U.S. foreign policy makers only named those nations that opposed U.S. policies, they argued, and these nations did not necessarily pose a broader threat to global security. In response to criticism of the rogue label, the Clinton administration replaced the term with "countries of concern."

In 2001, however, President George W. Bush adopted the term *rogue state*. After the terrorist attacks of September 11, 2001, the Bush administration formally defined *rogue states* in its National Security Strategy. According to the document, rogue states

> brutalize their own people and squander their national resources for the personal gain of the rulers; display no regard for international law, threaten their neighbors, and callously violate international treaties to which they are party; are determined to acquire weapons of mass destruction, along with other advanced military technology, to be used as threats or offensively to achieve the aggressive designs of these regimes; sponsor terrorism around the globe; and reject basic human values and hate the United States and everything for which it stands.

In his 2002 State of the Union address, President Bush singled out three countries—North Korea, Iran, and Iraq—as members of an "axis of evil." Although he did not use the term rogue when describing the threat posed by these nations, he used characteristics outlined in the National Security definition:

> North Korea is a regime arming with missiles and weapons of mass destruction, while starving its citizens. Iran aggressively pursues these weapons and exports terror, while an unelected few repress the Iranian people's hope for freedom. Iraq continues to flaunt its hostility toward America and to support terror. . . . States like these, and their terrorist allies, constitute an axis of evil, arming to threaten the peace of the world.

Critics of Bush administration foreign policy claim that labeling other nations rogue is hypocritical since the United States itself displays all the characteristics of the classic rogue state. The United States, they argue, has a history of aggressive foreign policy, ignores international law, and has relentlessly pursued weapons of mass destruction. Noam Chomsky, a political activist and professor at the Massachusetts Institute of Technology, has led the way in exposing what he views as American rogue behavior. The United States, he asserts, has even engaged in international terrorism:

> When the United States bombs Sudan and destroys half its pharmaceutical supply, that's international terrorism. When the United States bombed Libya, that's international terrorism. The U.S. war against Nicaragua—if we want to be kind to the United States—we could say it was international terrorism. A stronger, probably more accurate term would be outright aggression.

Members of the international community also increasingly view the United States as an aggressive rogue. American scholar Samuel Huntington maintains, "While the US regularly denounces various countries as 'rogue states,' in the eyes of many countries, it is becoming the rogue superpower." British playwright Harold Pinter, who won the Nobel Prize for literature in 2005, echoes Huntington's claim. Pinter asserts that the United States is the "most dangerous power the world has ever known—the authentic rogue state, but a rogue state of colossal military and economic might."

Some observers, however, believe that applying the label to any nation is simplistic and counterproductive. U.S. State Department official John Limbert claims, "The use of the term rogue state may make for a good soundbite, but it doesn't make for good policy." These analysts argue that the rogue-state label inhibits constructive dialogue among nations. "Naming and shaming countries such as Iraq, Iran, Libya and Cuba did not alter their behaviour," asserts foreign policy scholar Jennifer Rankin, "except perhaps to make them more hostile to the US." Not only does the rogue-state label "divert attention from the much more pressing question of how to deal with genuinely oppressive regimes," Rankin contends, it fails to accurately describe those nations labeled "rogue," including the United States. "All too often," she argues, "the doctrine of rogue states fails to distinguish between presidents and people. The many millions who make up the United States," she maintains, for example, "add up to more than their government's foreign policy." "Americans like things simple and broad," writes Smith of the rogue-nation label. "But in this instance," he continues, "adding a bit of complexity may well increase our security by allowing policy makers to distinguish the real from the illusionary challenges to the U.S. and the international community."

The authors of *Opposing Viewpoints: Rogue Nations* debate the rogue-nation label and other controversies concerning rogue nations in the following chapters: What Rogue Nations Pose a Serious Threat? What Threats Do Rogue Nations Pose? How Do Rogue Nations Threaten Human Rights? and How Should the Global Community Respond to Rogue Nations? As the debate over these countries illustrates, words are important. Foreign-policy makers are guided by the images that they have of nations that they believe pose a threat. Whether the rogue image will foster effective policies and increase global security continues to be hotly debated.

OPPOSING
VIEWPOINTS®
SERIES

CHAPTER 1

What Rogue Nations Pose a Serious Threat?

Chapter Preface

One of the enduring controversies in the debate over rogue nations is determining what states should be considered rogue. In defining what constitutes a rogue nation, most commentators today refer to the George W. Bush administration's 2002 National Security Strategy. According to this document, rogue nations are those that violate human rights, flout international law, pursue weapons of mass destruction, and sponsor terrorism. Those nations most often named rogues meet some or all of these criteria; they include Cuba, Iran, North Korea, Sudan, Syria, and even the United States. Some observers claim, however, that the criteria established by the National Security Strategy are subjective and incomplete. Weak and failing states, they argue, should also be considered rogue states because they pose a grave threat to global security. According to many analysts, these states provide a haven for terrorists. "Weak and failing states—and failed states—not only provide safe haven for terrorists," argues foreign-policy expert William M. Wise, "but also facilitate the planning, preparation and conduct of terrorist operations. On this basis alone . . . state failure represents a clear and present danger to the United States and its allies."

After the end of the Cold War, many new nations emerged. The international community assumed that these nations would provide for their people, exercise control over their territory, and cooperate with other nations. However, absent economic and military support from other countries, many of these new states began to fail. While strong states provide their people with economic opportunity and security, in weak states "the various infrastructural and economic networks that characterize strong states [deteriorate], corruption [increases] and autocrats often rule," writes Wise. Such states become plagued by armed insurgencies, civil disturbances, and discontent. "Violence is enduring [in these nations]," Wise maintains, "with much of it directed against the government or regime." In addition to having internal domestic problems, a weak or failed nation is "utterly incapable of sustaining itself as a member of the international community," add foreign policy analysts Gerald B. Helman and Steven R. Ratner. These characteristics—internal weakness and isolation from the international community—make weak and failed states an ideal environment for terrorists.

Weak and failed states provide several advantages for terrorists, argue foreign policy scholars Ray Takeyh and Nikolas Gvodsev. These states provide terrorists with land on which they can, without interference, construct training complexes, store arms, and build communication facilities. Since law enforcement is often ineffectual or nonexistent in weak and failed states, terrorists can raise funds through criminal activities such as smuggling and drug trafficking. Weak and failed states also create pools of potential recruits among the discontented and unemployed. Terrorists in such states can obtain legitimate travel documents and military hardware. Finally, because failed states retain the outward symbols of sovereignty, they can also prevent other nations from conducting counterterrorist operations within their borders. "Failed states may be notoriously unable to control their own territory, but they remain loath to allow access to any other states to do the same," argue Takeyh and Gvodsev. Scholars at the Yale Center for the Study of Globalization conclude, "The international community must develop a comprehensive, multilateral response that prevents stumbling states from becoming lost, or host of dangerous causes."

Whether weak and failed states should be considered rogue nations because they provide a haven for terrorists is central to national security debates. The authors in the following chapter explore the question of what countries should be considered rogue nations. Correctly identifying such nations is vital to enhancing international security.

> *"Iran's intimate relationship with international terrorism, and its potential for catastrophic proliferation suggest that ... [it] would constitute a truly global threat."*

Iran Poses a Serious Threat

Ilan Berman

Iran's nuclear program makes the nation a serious threat, argues Ilan Berman in the following viewpoint. Nations in the Middle East that fear Iran's growing nuclear power are forming bilateral military agreements with Iran that threaten their relations with the United States, he maintains. Moreover, Berman claims, Iran's clerical military regime has strong terrorist connections, increasing the possibility that Iran might arm terrorists with nuclear weapons. Berman is vice president of the American Foreign Policy Council, a public policy think tank.

As you read, consider the following questions:

1. What evidence does Berman cite that Iran's nuclear program is intended to do more than supply electricity?

Ilan Berman, "Nuclear Capabilities of Iran," Statement of Ilan Berman, Vice President, American Foreign Policy Council, before the Committee on Senate Homeland Security and Governmental Affairs Subcommittee on Federal Financial Management, Government Information and International Security, November 15, 2005.

2. According to the author, why do Iran's atomic advances hold the potential to touch off a dangerous regional arms race?

3. What will help preserve U.S. coalition solidarity in the Middle East, in the author's view?

Since August 2002, when an Iranian opposition group disclosed information about two previously-unknown clandestine Iranian nuclear facilities, the world has woken up to the frightening possibility that the radical regime now in power in Tehran may soon possess a nuclear arsenal. More than three years later, much is still unknown about Iran's nuclear program. Yet compelling evidence suggests that Iran's efforts are much more than simply an attempt to develop an additional source of energy.

Iran's Nuclear Ambitions

- Iran's atomic endeavor is massive in scope, encompassing as many as two-dozen sites scattered throughout the country, and focusing on both uranium enrichment and plutonium conversion. This represents a far greater effort than is necessary simply for the generation of supplemental electricity, the avowed goal of Iran's nuclear program.

- Like its chemical and biological weapons programs and its expanding arsenal of ballistic missiles, Iran's nuclear program has been placed under the direct control of the regime's clerical army, the Pasdaran. This strongly suggests that Iran's atomic effort is intended for distinctly military applications.

- Iran has engaged in a pattern of diplomatic obfuscation and deception designed to prevent full oversight of its nuclear processes. Tehran has managed to circumvent its December 2003 decision to sign on to the Additional Protocol to the Nuclear Nonproliferation Treaty (NPT), which permits snap inspections and invasive monitoring of segments of its nuclear sector by the IAEA [International Atomic Energy Agency] and has "sanitized," moved and otherwise hidden suspect sites from international inspectors, preventing effective oversight of its nuclear efforts.

- Iran has rejected proposals that would have provided it simply with sufficient nuclear capabilities for energy development. These include a February 2005 European offer to supply the Islamic Republic with light-water nuclear reactors suitable for electricity generation, but not for the production of weapons-grade uranium. . . .

The international response to this nuclear challenge has been woefully inadequate. Since mid-2003, when the IAEA first found that Iran had failed to meet its obligations under the NPT, the European Union has been engaged in a complicated, halting set of diplomatic negotiations with the Islamic Republic. These talks, spearheaded by the "EU-3"—Great Britain, France and Germany—have unsuccessfully attempted to secure a lasting Iranian freeze on uranium enrichment in exchange for economic and political incentives (including accession to the World Trade Organization and the provision of aeronautical components for Iran's aging fleet of airliners).

Since February 2005, the [George W.] Bush administration has thrown its weight behind this diplomatic initiative, engaging in nuclear dialogue with Iran via the EU-3. It has done so despite President Bush's declaration that the United States "will not tolerate" a nuclear-armed Iran, and notwithstanding serious structural flaws with the scope and objectives of the negotiating process itself.

Regional Impact of a Nuclear Iran

Iran's atomic endeavor holds the potential to dramatically alter the strategic balance in the Middle East. Already, Iranian advances have begun to change the political climate in the Persian Gulf. [Since 2000], in an indicator of mounting concern over Iran's expanding nuclear and ballistic missile capabilities, a number of regional states have signed bilateral military agreements with the Islamic Republic. Over time, such pacts can be expected to make the Persian Gulf less and less hospitable to the United States, as regional nations seek a modus vivendi with a nearly-nuclear Iran.

Likewise, Iran's atomic advances hold the potential to touch off a dangerous regional arms race, as neighboring states accelerate their efforts to acquire a counterweight to Iranian capabilities. The beginnings of such a trend are already becoming visible: In October 2003, the *Washington Times* revealed details of a secret agreement between Saudi Arabia and Pakistan granting Riyadh [Saudi Arabia's capital] access to Pakistani nuclear technologies in exchange for cheap, steady supplies of Saudi crude. Similarly, discoveries of trace plutonium at Egyptian nuclear facilities have deepened international suspicions about the nuclear aspirations of the government of Egyptian President Hosni Mubarak. A nuclear Iran can also be expected to pose a major proliferation threat. The Pasdaran is the Iranian regime's principal point of contact with terrorist groups such as Hezbollah. Its control of the Iranian nuclear program raises the possibility that Iran's nuclear advances could translate into substantial terrorist gains. Indeed, the Islamic Republic's provision of large quantities of indigenously-made "Fajr-5", short-range missiles and artillery rockets, to Hezbollah over the past three years suggests that this represents a very real danger. Compounding such worries, Iran's new, hard-line president, Mahmoud Ahmadinejad, . . . confirmed publicly that his government is prepared to provide nuclear technology to any number of other Muslim states. The greatest casualties of Iran's nuclear progress, however, are likely to be internal forces opposed to the current Iranian regime. Armed with atomic weaponry, Iran will have far greater

THE SHAPE...

OF THINGS...

TO COME ...

IRAN

Robert Ariail. PoliticalCartoons.com. Reproduced by permission.

ability to quash domestic dissent with impunity, without concern over decisive international retaliation much the same way China did in its brutal, bloody suppression of student protests in Tiananmen Square in 1989. A nuclear capability therefore can be expected to substantially dim prospects for internal transformation within the Islamic Republic, and to provide the Iranian regime with a new lease on life.

Toward an American Approach

How should the United States respond to this challenge? The fundamental problem is that Iran's "nuclear clock" is ticking much faster than its "regime change" clock. Altering that equation should be the starting point for any serious American strategy. Fortunately, the United States has several tools by which it can delay Iran's nuclear ambitions, and mitigate their impact on the Middle East:

International cooperation. For the moment, U.S. and foreign intelligence services are in agreement that Iran's nuclear program has not yet reached a "point of no return" (although there are substantial differences of opinion over exactly when

Iran will cross that threshold). And because Iran still depends on foreign assistance for its nuclear endeavor, the United States can work with its international partners to influence the pace at which Iran progresses toward the "bomb." As part of this process, Washington can and should pressure countries in Europe and Asia to: impose stricter monitoring on sales of potential dual-use technologies to Iran; create greater domestic penalties for WMD [weapons of mass destruction]-related exports to Iran, and; more stringently enforce existing domestic legislation prohibiting WMD-related trade.

Counterproliferation. Since its establishment in May 2003, the Bush administration's most important counterproliferation effort, the Proliferation Security Initiative (PSI), has emerged as a major strategic success. Today, the PSI encompasses more than 60 countries in one form or another, and can be credited with successfully curtailing much of North Korea's missile trade with the Middle East. So far, however, the PSI has not been adapted to comprehensively address the contemporary threat from Iran. The White House should make it a priority to do so. Through closer cooperation with like-minded states in the Persian Gulf and Eastern Mediterranean on intelligence-sharing and interdiction, the United States has the ability to complicate Iran's acquisition of WMD and ballistic missile technologies from foreign suppliers, and to simultaneously stem the onward proliferation of these capabilities to rogue states or terrorist groups.

Gulf defense. Over the past several years, fears of Iran's expanding capabilities have begun to drive many of the Persian Gulf states toward accommodation with the Islamic Republic. Preserving U.S. coalition solidarity in the region requires the provision of local antidotes to the Iranian strategic threat. Robust deployments of American theater missile defenses among the Gulf Cooperation Council (GCC) states, for example, will help blunt Iran's ability to engage in nuclear blackmail against those nations. A deepening of Washington's bilateral military dialogue with individual Gulf states likewise might lessen regional dependence on Iran. So would the creation of a formal American security architecture capable of providing countries currently threatened by Iran with concrete mutual defense guarantees.

It is important to recognize, however, that while these steps may help to complicate Iran's efforts (and mitigate their regional impact), they cannot end them. Iranian policymakers have embraced the idea of nuclear weapons as central to ensuring regime stability, and to "preempting" the possibility of military action on the part of the United States. Moreover, the Iranian nuclear endeavor actually appears to enjoy broad support among ordinary citizens, irrespective of their attitudes toward the ruling regime in Tehran.

The ultimate question, therefore, revolves around regime character. The danger of a nuclear Iran does not stem from the Iranian nuclear program itself. Rather, it comes from the nature of the regime that will ultimately wield those weapons. Iran's intimate relationship with international terrorism, and its potential for catastrophic proliferation, suggests that an Islamic Republic armed with nuclear weapons would constitute a truly global threat.

As a result, the United States must do more than simply deter and contain Iran. It must also focus its energies upon means by which it can spur a fundamental transformation of that regime.

VIEWPOINT 2

> *"The Iranian regime is not invulnerable."*

The Iranian Threat Is Overstated

Dariush Zahedi and Omid Memarian

The threat posed by Iran is overstated, claim Iranian-American political scientist Dariush Zahedi and Iranian journalist Omid Memarian in the following viewpoint. In fact, the authors argue, Iran has internal weaknesses: a poor economy, discontented minorities, and a widespread drug abuse problem. If Iran were to pursue aggressive policies toward the United States and other nations, its weak economy would likely collapse. Thus, the wisest course for Iran will obviously be to cooperate with the international community.

As you read, consider the following questions:

1. According to Zahedi and Memarian, what motivates Iranian president Mahmoud Ahmadinejad's bravado?
2. In the authors' opinion, under what circumstances might Ahmadinejad welcome an American or Israeli strike on Iran's nuclear facilities?

Dariush Zahedi and Omid Memarian, "A Firebrand in a House of Cards," *New York Times*, January 12, 2006. Reprinted with permission.

3. What will happen to the Iranian economy if the United States refers Iran's nuclear file to the UN Security Council, in the authors' view?

In defying international monitors and breaking the seals on its nuclear facilities, Iran seems to be courting confrontation. But Western leaders would do well to consider what [Iran's] President Mahmoud Ahmadinejad's bravado really says about Iran's likely posture in the region and at the nuclear talks that are scheduled to resume at the end of January [2006]. To continue down the path of conflict could be very costly, both for the regional interests of the United States and most of all, for the territorial integrity of Iran.

Mr. Ahmadinejad is surely motivated by ideology and the desire to solidify the position of the security faction within Iran's ruling elite. But he also appears to be acting on the perception that the United States is in a position of considerable, indeed unprecedented, weakness. America's military is overstretched in Iraq and Afghanistan, and Washington has focused on monitoring North Korea's nuclear program rather than Iran's. If threatened, Iran could wreak havoc in Afghanistan, Iraq, Lebanon and Israel. These observations may lead Mr. Ahmadinejad to an incorrect assessment of Iran's strength relative to any American threat.

Iran's Domestic Frailties

In fact, Iran has serious domestic frailties, including a shaky economy and its attendant unemployment and popular resentment, not to mention soaring levels of drug abuse and a brain drain. But President Ahmanadinejad no doubt takes comfort not only in his belief in divine protection but also in the knowledge that Shiite religious parties aligned with Iran are now the dominant political forces in Iraq, while the American public hardly seems amenable to waging another war in the region. Moreover, Mr. Ahmadinejad very likely believes that the best way to guard against regime change from with

A New Generation of Clerics Want Better Relations with America

There is every reason to believe that [Iran's] clerical establishment, despite its stale, shrill anti-American rhetoric, would jump at the chance at opening economic ties with the United States. It would be an enormous coup for it to accomplish what Iran's reformists have been trying so hard to do for more than a decade. Already the clerics have co-opted the rhetoric of reform in order to appease the population and thereby cling to power: A new generation of clerics now speaks openly of a steady transition to full democracy. Extremism and militancy in the clerical hierarchy are gradually giving way to moderation and pragmatism.

Reza Aslan, Nation, *February 28, 2005*

out is to emulate North Korea by swiftly advancing Iran's nuclear capacity.

The new president also surely knows that even if Iran's nuclear dossier is referred to the United Nations Security Council [it was, in February 2006], meaningful multilateral sanctions against the Islamic Republic will most likely be vetoed by Russia or China. Flush with petrodollars [oil revenues], Iran has become a major purchaser of Russian technology, including roughly $1 billion worth of allegedly defensive weapons that Moscow ... agreed to sell to Tehran. Meanwhile, China, seizing on Iran as a key producer of oil and gas not beholden to the United States, has quickly emerged as one of Iran's largest trading partners.

Given this favorable strategic picture, Mr. Ahmadinejad might even welcome an American or Israeli strike on Iran's nuclear facilities. Tehran could then retaliate against American and Israeli interests by mobilizing its Shiite allies in Iraq, the

Persian Gulf countries and Lebanon—or even by making common cause with some Sunni rivals. All the while, Mr. Ahmadinejad's faction in government would make full use of the war footing to marginalize its rivals at home and crush the remnants of Iran's civil society.

Iran's Vulnerabilities

But the Iranian regime is not invulnerable and Washington knows this. Just as Iran can use the Shiite card to create mischief in the region, the United States could manipulate ethnic and sectarian tensions in Iran, which has significant, largely Sunni, minority populations along its borders.

Many of Iran's ethnic and religious minorities see themselves as victims of discrimination, and they have not been effectively integrated into Iranian economic, political or cultural life. Some two million disgruntled Arabs reside mainly in the oil- and gas-rich province of Khuzestan. The United States could make serious trouble for Tehran by providing financial, logistical and moral support to Arab secessionists in that province. Other aggrieved Iranian minorities would be emboldened by the Arabs' example—for example, the Kurds and the Baluchis, or even the Azeris (though the Azeris, being Shiites, are better integrated into Iranian society). A simple spark could suffice to set off centrifugal explosions.

Furthermore, the plummeting Iranian economy will only worsen if the United States succeeds in referring Iran's nuclear file to the Security Council, whether or not meaningful sanctions follow. Such a referral would accelerate capital flight, deal a blow to the country's already collapsing stock market, devastate its hitherto booming real estate market, and wipe out the savings of a large part of the middle class. It would also most likely result in galloping inflation, hurting Iran's dispossessed, whom the Ahmadinejad administration claims to represent.

Avoiding Conflict

In light of these ominous possibilities, both Mr. Ahmadinejad and Mr. Bush would do well to avoid overplaying their hands. They should take a leaf from the book not of Ayatollah Ruhollah Khomeini the ideologue, but of Ayatollah Khomeini the pragmatic politician. Like Mr. Ahmadinejad, Ayatollah Khomeini argued that the "Zionist entity" should be wiped off the map. But he chose regime preservation over ideology when he ended the Iran-Iraq war and even bought weapons from Israel.

Iran should endeavor to regain the trust of the international community by engaging in compromise, and the United States should allow this compromise to be sufficiently face-saving for Iran's ruling elite. To regain the confidence of the international community, Iran should accept the Russian offer to process Iranian uranium gas into fuel and voluntarily stop, for a specified time, insisting on its right to do so at home.

In return, the United States should lift its unilateral sanctions from Iran. These sanctions, which include a ban on the sale of aircraft and spare parts to Iran, have absolutely no effect on the regime's nuclear capacity, but they harm Iranian civilians.

Today the incentive for both sides to step away from the brink of conflict is even greater than it was at the end of the Iran-Iraq war. If the United States responds to a perceived Iranian threat by exploiting Iran's ethnic, sectarian and economic cleavages, it is not just the Islamic Republic that will be threatened—Iran itself could be dismembered as well.

> "[North Korea is a] dangerous nation
> ... whose only source of power ... has
> been to create as many threats as it can
> to the peace and security of the region."

North Korea Threatens International Security

Bruce Bennett

In the following viewpoint Bruce Bennett argues that North Korea is an aggressive, totalitarian regime whose goal is to conquer South Korea. Because North Korea cannot succeed in a conventional war against U.S.-supported South Korean forces, North Korean leaders intend to use nuclear, chemical, and biological weapons, he claims. Such aggression toward South Korea would adversely impact all of Northeast Asia, the authors contend. Moreover, Bennett asserts, North Korea could sell nuclear weapons to terrorists who might use them against the United States and its allies. Bennett is a senior policy analyst at the Rand Corporation, a public policy think tank.

As you read, consider the following questions:

1. In Bennett's opinion, how was the American Civil War different from the civil war between North and South Korea?

Bruce Bennett, "N. Korea's Threat to S. Korea," United Press International, March 7, 2003. Reproduced by permission.

2. According to the author, why do North Korea's outdated weapons provide no reason to relax?

3. Why does Korean reunification remain unlikely, in the author's view?

In 1915, 50 years after the last shots were fired in the American Civil War, few people could imagine the resumption of hostilities between the North and South. Today, almost 50 years after the end of the civil war between North and South Korea, growing numbers of young people in the South similarly can't imagine a new war with their "brothers and sisters" in the North.

But while America's Civil War ended with the preservation of the United States, Korea's led only to an angry armistice between two hostile states facing each other at gunpoint. Despite this, for growing numbers of South Koreans, the 400,000 deaths their nation suffered at the hands of their northern brethren in the 1950s are merely words in history books. This is why many young South Koreans today seem convinced that an attack from North Korea is extraordinarily unlikely.

A Grave Threat

This belief is at odds with reality: Even though it has the 13th largest economy in the world and a strong military, South Korea has much to fear from its dangerous northern neighbor, which is armed with weapons of mass destruction—probably including nuclear weapons—and which, even more frighteningly, has developed a specific strategy for using them.

Some military experts say the North Korean military is far inferior to South Korean and American forces, and therefore is not a serious threat. They rightly note that while North Korea has a military force of more than 1 million, most of its conventional weapons and equipment were designed in the 1950s and 1960s—making them old, hard to maintain and prone to breakdowns.

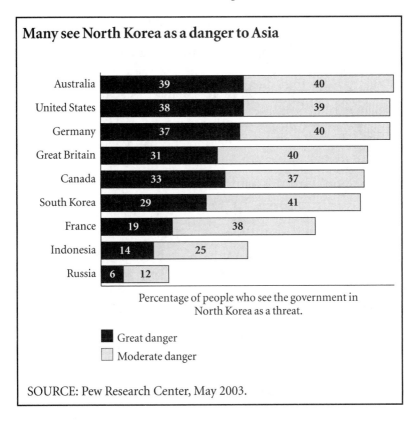

Many see North Korea as a danger to Asia

Percentage of people who see the government in North Korea as a threat.

■ Great danger
☐ Moderate danger

SOURCE: Pew Research Center, May 2003.

But far from being a reason to relax, this situation may in fact be the foundation for the current grave threat against South Korea. It was the basis, say some of these same experts, for a decision made about 20 years ago by North Korea that it could not compete with the modernizing South Korean and U.S. military forces, and that it would instead emphasize weapons of mass destruction.

A Three-Tiered Strategy

According to these experts, North Korea seems to have opted for a three-tiered strategy that involves using weapons of mass destruction to catastrophically damage South Korean and U.S. forces to the point where the outdated North Korean equipment and weapons might still be effective.

The strategy's components are as follows:

- Against South Korean and American battlefield forces, North Korea has emphasized artillery with chemical weapons, and built a huge arsenal of each.

- Against the nearby South Korean capital, Seoul, and ground force reserves behind the battlefield, North Korea has emphasized long-range artillery with chemical weapons, and special forces with biological weapons.

- Against rear area and off-peninsula targets, North Korea has emphasized ballistic missiles with chemical weapons and special forces with biological weapons, and the development of nuclear weapons.

The North Koreans could cause tremendous damage whether or not this strategy works. For example, one battery of North Korean 240-mm multiple rocket launchers fired into Seoul can deliver roughly a ton of chemical weapons, which, according to various accounts, could kill or injure thousands or tens of thousands. North Korea has many such batteries.

In addition, North Korean special forces teams might each spray several kilograms of anthrax in Seoul, leaving tens to hundreds of thousands of people infected, many of whom would die unless properly treated.

A North Korean nuclear weapon fired into Seoul might cause damage similar to that of the nuclear weapon detonated on Hiroshima [Japan] in World War II, which left some 70,000 dead and 75,000 injured.

It is generally believed that if North Korea has only one or two nuclear weapons, the regime will likely withhold them unless it faces certain defeat and destruction. But if it builds five or 10 nuclear weapons, as it may soon do, it may be inclined to use some against South Korea early in the conflict to demonstrate its power and rapidly achieve some military objectives. It might also sell some of these weapons to terrorists who could try to use them against the United States or its allies.

A Different Outcome

The end of the American Civil War reunified the United States and ended a terrible crisis for our country. In contrast, the armed, fragile, jittery 50-year hiatus in the civil war between the two Koreas has yielded the opposite. It has created a modern, prosperous, ever-evolving state in the south—a valuable member of the world economic community—and a totalitarian, aggressive, and dangerous nation in the north, whose only source of power on the world stage has been to create as many threats as it can to the peace and security of the region, and then push them as far as possible in order to attract attention and exact concessions.

North Korea is a police state led by a dictator who has a specific strategy—and an often-stated intent—to conquer South Korea. Believing anything else is an illusion, and the latest generation of South Koreans does that at their peril— and at the peril of the other nations in Northeast Asia, which would all suffer from such a war.

While this grave risk might be healed by the eventual peaceful reunification of the two Koreas, it is unlikely that will happen as long as [North Korea's leader] Kim Jong Il's preferred method of "diplomacy" involves threatening South Korea and some of his other neighbors with weapons of mass destruction.

> "The Korean conflict is over, but Cold War warriors refuse to accept this reality because they need a 'threat.'"

The North Korean Threat Is a Myth

Carlton Meyer

North Korea's poor economy, decrepit military, and diplomatic isolation make the nation a feeble threat, claims Carlton Meyer in the following viewpoint. Although Russia and China were North Korea's allies during the Cold War, they now trade heavily with South Korea and thus have a strong interest in protecting the South from the North, he maintains. Meyer argues that the U.S. military presence in South Korea actually poses a greater threat to the region's stability than does North Korea. If the United States withdrew its forces, North Korea would feel less threatened and would act less aggressively, he asserts. Meyer served with the U.S. Marine Corps in Asia.

As you read, consider the following questions:

1. What evidence does Meyer provide of South Korea's military superiority?

Carlton Meyer, "The Mythical North Korean Threat," www.g2mil.com, 2003. Reproduced by permission.

2. According to the author, what impediment must be removed before North Korea will progress with peace talks?

3. What evidence does the author provide that North and South Korea are reconnecting?

The Korean conflict is over, but Cold War warriors refuse to accept this reality because they need a "threat." In 1994, the military-industrialist [complex] worked the media and politicians into a war hysteria which almost caused President Clinton to order air strikes in North Korea. In his book, *Hazardous Duty*, retired Colonel David Hackworth describes his trip to Korea in which he uncovered this phony threat. Fortunately, former President Jimmy Carter heard the war drums and flew to North Korea as a private citizen and ended the phantom crisis.

South Korean Superiority

When Pentagon officials talk about the need to maintain a "two-war" capability, they often refer to Korea. This is absurd since South Korea can crush North Korea without American help. North Korea's million-man army may look impressive on paper, but remember that Iraq had a million-man army, which also had modern equipment, combat experience, and plenty of fuel [and was defeated by America and its allies in 2003].

In contrast, North Korean soldiers suffer from malnutrition and rarely train due to a scarcity of fuel and ammo. Most North Korean soldiers could not attack because they are needed to defend the entire DMZ [demilitarized zone] and coastal approaches (they remember the 1950 landing at Inchon) while entire divisions must remain throughout North Korea to fend off heliborne offensives, food riots, and probable coups.

On the other hand, the entire 700,000 man South Korean active duty army can be devoted to the defense of Seoul [South

Korea's capital]. The modern South Korean army is backed by over 5,000,000 well-trained reservists who can be called to duty in hours. South Korea has twice the population of the North, thirty times its economic power, and spends three times more on its military each year. South Korean military equipment is first class whereas most of the North Korean military equipment is over 30 years old and much is inoperable due to a lack of maintenance. If war broke out, South Korea has a massive industrial capacity and $94 billion in foreign currency reserves to sustain a war, while North Korea has no industry and no money. As a result, South Korea is roughly five times more powerful than North Korea.

In the Event of an Unlikely Attack

If North Korea insanely attacked, the South Koreans would fight on mountainous and urban terrain which heavily favors defense, and complete air superiority would shoot up anything the North Koreans put on the road. Assuming the North Koreans could start up a thousand of their old tanks and armored vehicles, they cannot advance through the mountainous DMZ. The South Koreans have fortified, mined, and physically blocked all avenues through these mountains, and it would take North Korean infantry and engineers weeks to clear road paths while under fire.

The North Korean military could gain a few thousand meters with human wave assaults into minefields and concrete fortifications. However, these attacks would bog down from heavy casualties, and a lack of food and ammo resupply. Fighting would be bloody as thousands of South Korean and American troops and civilians suffer from North Korean artillery and commando attacks. Nevertheless, the North Korean army would be unable to break through or move supplies forward. Even if North Korea magically broke through, all military analysts scoff at the idea that the North Koreans could bridge large rivers or move tons of supplies forward while under attack from American airpower.

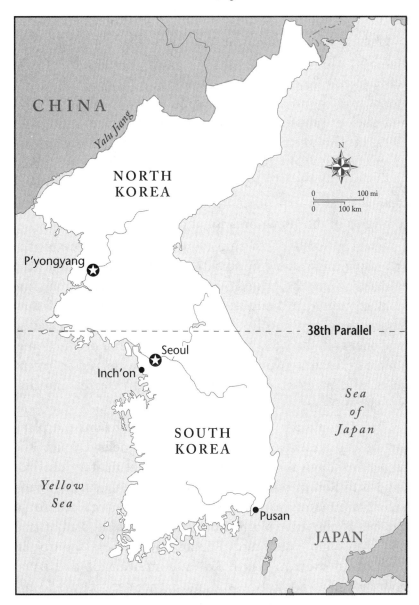

A Weak, Unsupported Military

It is important to remember that the last Korean war involved Chinese forces supported by North Koreans with the latest Soviet equipment and supplies. China and Russia no longer aid

North Korea and trade openly with South Korea. Thousands of Chinese soldiers guard the Yalu River [that separates China and North Korea] to prevent crossings by starving North Koreans. North Korean soldiers no longer train for war, but spend most hours harvesting crops, while their old aircraft and ancient tanks sit idle from a lack of fuel and parts. In 1999, Lt. Gen. Patrick Hughes, head of the Defense Intelligence Agency, told Congress that discipline in the North Korean army had collapsed, and that refugees report soldiers stealing food at gun point. Nighttime satellite pictures reveal few lights in the North because of a lack of electricity.

Even if North Korea employs a few crude nuclear weapons, using them would be suicidal since it would invite instant retaliation from the United States. North Korea lacks the technical know-how to build an Intercontinental Ballistic Missile, despite the hopes and lies from the National Missile Defense proponents in the USA. North Korea's industrial production is almost zero, over two million people have starved in recent years, and millions of homeless nomads threaten internal revolution.

The US military ignores this reality and retains old plans for the deployment of 450,000 GIs to help defend South Korea, even though the superior South Korean military can halt any North Korean offensive without help from a single American soldier. American forces are not even required for a counter-offensive. A North Korean attack would stall after a few intense days and South Korean forces would soon be in position to overrun North Korea. American air and naval power along with logistical and intelligence support would ensure the rapid collapse of the North Korean army.

However, South Korean leaders would be distressed about economic losses and the cost of occupying the North. They would have little incentive to overrun North Korea quickly if 450,000 free spending American GIs with billions of dollars in American military aid were on the way. Rather than quickly overrunning the North, South Korean leaders may demobilize some units to restart its economy. Hopefully, Americans will realize that something is wrong when infantrymen from Kansas are deployed to invade North Korea while infantrymen from Seoul are sent home. Perhaps they will recall the logic of President Lyndon Johnson who said in 1964 that he was "not about to send American boys nine or ten thousand miles from home to do what Asian boys ought to be doing themselves." If South Koreans are unwilling to defend their nation from poverty stricken cousins from the North, why should Americans defend them? The USA imports no vital resources from Korea; the consumer items imported from South Korea are readily available elsewhere.

The Cold War Is Over

Chinese participation is extremely unlikely since China is busy with its free enterprise transformation while ensuring domestic tranquility. In fact, stopping thousands of starving North Korean refugees from crossing their border has become a major problem, although the Chinese refuse to spend any of their billions of dollars in US trade surpluses to purchase food for their old ally. Korea has no natural resources which interest China, and Chinese support would cause a major war with powerful South Korea, the United States, and probably Japan and Taiwan. On the other hand, a prosperous Korea provides a buffer against China's traditional enemy—Japan.

The US Army must adapt to the end of the Cold War in Asia and stop wasting millions of dollars on new military construction projects in Korea. Second, the North Koreans have stated that the 37,000 American troops must go before peace talks can progress. (Imagine how South Korea would feel if 37,000 Russian troops were based in North Korea.) Many South Koreans know that American troops are no longer needed and anti-American base protests are common. . . .

The chance of a Korean war is extremely unlikely. North Korean leaders realize they have no hope of success without major backing from China or Russia. The previous South Korean President, Kim Dae Jung, encouraged peace and visited North Korea. The two countries are reconnecting rail lines and sent a combined team to the Olympics. Even the United States is providing $500 million a year in food to the starving North Koreans. The new South Korean President, Roh Moohyan was elected on a peace platform and suggested US troops may be gone within ten years.

It may take many years for the two Koreas to unite, meanwhile the USA can contribute to peace and save billions of dollars by starting a withdrawal of forces. The US Army can increase its ability to deploy expeditionary forces in Asia by cutting infrastructure in Korea. . . . The USA already has a huge logistical infrastructure in Japan, Hawaii and Guam, it doesn't need bases in Korea. American forces should continue to train with South Korea, but the $5 billion a year military base subsidy to South Korea must end. Unfortunately, lying about the Korean situation has become a cornerstone of the Pentagon's effort to boost military spending beyond Cold War levels.

> *"Syria's nefarious activities pose grave concerns for the U.S. and its allies."*

Syria Poses a Threat

Ileana Ros-Lehtinen

According to U.S. Representative Ileana Ros-Lehtinen in the following viewpoint, Syria's weapons capabilities, its support for global terrorism, and its connection to other rogue nations make the nation a grave threat to the United States and its allies. Foreign investors, including U.S. companies, provide Syria with the funds it uses to develop chemical, biological, and nuclear weapons, she maintains. In addition, Ros-Lehtinen asserts, Syria is supplying terrorist groups such as Hezbollah with arms and is hiding weapons of mass destruction in Lebanon.

As you read, consider the following questions:

1. According to CIA director William Webster, how have Western European companies directly contributed to Syria's weapons programs?

2. What diseases do sources claim Syria can weaponize?

3. With what rogue nation does the author claim Syria is linked?

Ileana Ros-Lehtinen, "Statement by Hon. Ileana Ros-Lehtinen, Chair Subcommittee on the Middle East and Central Asia Committee on International Relations U.S. House of Representatives for Hearing: Syria: Implications for U.S. Security and Regional Stability-Part I," September 16, 2003.

The [U.S. House Subcommittee on the Middle East and Central Asia, Committee on International Relations] held an oversight hearing to assess the impact that foreign investment in Iran's energy infrastructure has had on the Iranian regime's ability to finance its nuclear program, its development of long-range ballistic missiles, and its continued sponsoring of terrorist organizations.

Unfortunately we see a similar pattern emerging with respect to Syria.

Contributing to Syria's Weapons Build-Up

Foreign investors have readily answered Damascus' call for assistance, pumping billions of dollars into the regime's coffers through investments in the oil and gas sector, in turn, enabling Syria to expend its budgetary resources on its chemical and biological weapons projects, as well as its support for terrorist groups.

Even more disturbing is how Western European companies have directly contributed to Syria's weapons programs.

In 1989, former CIA [Central Intelligence Agency] Director, William Webster, told a Congressional panel that the CIA had determined foreign assistance was:

> of critical importance in allowing Syria to develop its chemical warfare capability. Western European firms were instrumental in supplying the required precursor chemicals and equipment. Without the provision of these key elements, Damascus would not have been able to produce chemical weapons.

Syria's Chemical Weapons

Since then, Syria has increased and diversified its weapons of mass destruction programs to present a serious threat to our allies and interests in the region.

An unclassified CIA report to Congress covering the period from January to June 2001, stated that "Syria sought chemical weapons related precursors and expertise from foreign sources, maintains a stockpile of the nerve agent sarin and appears to be trying to develop more toxic and persistent nerve agents."

Syria has reportedly manufactured varieties of aerial bombs containing chemical agents such as sarin gas. According to Russian intelligence, Syria has a stock of thousands of chemical aerial bombs that are carried by various types of planes. Syria also has several thousand tactical munitions, including rockets and artillery shells containing sarin gas.

Syria reportedly has three production facilities for chemical weapons but more disturbing, are reports that Syria is amassing chemical warheads for Scud missiles.

In January 2002, the CIA estimated that: "Syria has developed chemical weapons warheads for its Scuds" and that the intelligence community remains concerned about Syria's intentions regarding nuclear weapons.

Syria reportedly produces 30 Scud-C missiles per year at an underground facility, and many Western analysts agree that these Syrian Scud-C's, originally purchased from North Korea, are being armed for long-range chemical weapons delivery.

Syrian sources have publicly confirmed the test firing of Scud-B and Scud-C missiles with weaponized chemical agents.

Further, recent public reports indicate that Syria has purchased and already possesses ballistic/cruise missiles that can carry warheads with clusters of chemical and biological agents.

In addition to mobile brigades, Syria has reportedly constructed hardened silos and a network of tunnels to hide its longer-range missiles.

Syria's Biological Weapons

With respect to Syria's biological weapons program, the Center for Scientific Studies and Research in Damascus has been reported to be the primary site for both Syria's biological and chemical programs—not to mention the procurement of dual-

The Threat from Syria

The threat from Syria looms large. Until Damascus abandons its state sponsorship of terrorism, WMD-[weapons of mass destruction] programs, steady build-up of offensive and defensive missile systems, and active weapons proliferation, it will remain a significant cause for concern.

Claremont Institute, MissileThreat.com, 2005, www.missilethreat.com.

use chemical and biological technology and equipment from various European and South Asian countries.

The Center's published studies point to work with germs and proteins, and report that the Center's scientists have trained in France in the fields of toxicology and virology.

Various sources have reported that Syria possesses, and can weaponize, anthrax and cholera.

It has also been reported that the smallpox virus was delivered to Syria from Russia for bioweapons development and that the Syrian regime is investigating the use of another pathogen related to the bubonic plague.

Scholarly and media sources state that production facilities for chemical weapons in the Aleppo area, and at other sites, also include biological weapons facilities.

While some assessments do not place Syria's biological weapons programs beyond the research and development stage, the intentions of the Syrian regime with respect to its work with biological agents was made abundantly clear in April 2000 in a lengthy article published by the Syrian Defense Minister.

In this article entitled: "Biological Germ Warfare: A New and Effective Method in Modern Warfare" the Syrian Defense Minister spoke about the military's plan to integrate biological weapons in its tactical and strategic arsenals.

Syria's Nuclear Potential

However, the current and potential threats posed by the regime in Damascus do not end with chemical and biological weapons.

Both Syria's current research reactor, provided by China, and one light-water reactor that Russia has reportedly agreed to provide Syria, are under the supervision and scrutiny of the International Atomic Energy Agency.

However, there are reports that Damascus has attempted to obtain assistance on further developing its nuclear infrastructure from Argentina and China.

There are persistent rumors of a covert nuclear weapons program, along with reports of planes returning from Syria to Iraq in 2002, with foam-producing systems, which could be used for uranium-enrichment.

These, combined with Syria's recent agreement with Russia concerning close cooperation on nuclear power, raise grave questions regarding the Syrian regime's true objectives on the nuclear front.

The same linkage former CIA Director Webster warned us about in 1989 regarding the role of foreign assistance in developing Syria's chemical weapons, applies to Syria's nuclear intentions today.

Thus, it is imperative to keep in mind President Bush's statement in his January 29, 2002, State of the Union address. The President declared that the United States would work "to deny terrorists and their state sponsors the materials, technology, and expertise to make and deliver weapons of mass destruction [WMD]."

Supporting Terrorists

In themselves, Syria's nefarious activities pose grave concerns for the U.S. and its allies. However, the magnitude of the threat increases dramatically when placed in the context of Syria's continued support for global terrorism and its relationship with other pariah states.

Public U.S. and foreign sources assess that there has been a qualitative increase in Syria's role in arms supply to terrorist groups such as Hizballah. There are reports that Syria has recently begun supplying extended range rockets from its own production to Hizballah.

We have also received information from public sources indicating that Syria is using Lebanon to hide WMD and to serve as a trans-shipment point for weapons to terrorist groups, given that the coalition victory in Iraq closed many of their usual transport routes.

There is also increased cooperation between Syria and other rogue regimes such as Iran.

Throughout the 1990s, delivery of missiles and related cargo was done in coordination with the Iranian regime.

On May 29, 2003, Syrian Deputy Prime Minister and Foreign Minister described the bilateral relations between Syria and Iran as being in the best shape ever. He noted that coordination between Syria and Iran is based on long experience and joint interests.

Unfortunately, just as ties between Iran and Syria appear to be strengthening, governments focused on appeasing these two terrorist regimes are also expanding their ties with Iran and Syria.

As I noted at the beginning of my statement, the scope and nature of foreign investments in Syria, almost directly mirror the pattern established with Iran.

Perhaps even more troubling, however, are the investments of U.S. companies in Syria. I am deeply concerned that American companies continue to sign multi-billion dollar deals to invest in Syria's oil and gas sector. Worse yet, they are reportedly joining hundreds of other types of U.S. companies doing business in Syria.

We must work to deny Syria all resources and abilities to expand its WMD capabilities. The U.S. must use every tool at its disposal to confront this threat.

I believe the Syria Accountability and Lebanese Sovereignty Restoration Act, which has accumulated over 250 cosponsors, is such a response. This Act represents a long overdue effort to hold Syria accountable for its sponsorship of terrorism, its development of weapons of mass destruction, and its ongoing occupation of Lebanon, by toughening economic and other sanctions against Syria.[1]

On May 11, 2002, Secretary of State [Colin] Powell warned the Syrian leader that he "will find that he is on the wrong side of history" if he does not, among other priorities, move against terrorism and discourage the spread of weapons of mass destruction.

It appears to me that, for over two decades and, particularly since the September 11th [terrorist] attacks, Syria's overall actions have not been those of a state that shares our commitment to non-proliferation and combating terrorism.

---

1. The bill became law on December 12, 2003.

"There is a significant danger that the black market will put Pakistani nukes ... in terrorist hands."

Pakistan Threatens Nuclear Security

Graham Allison

Pakistan's nuclear program poses two serious threats to global security, argues Graham Allison in the following viewpoint. First, he asserts, terrorists could obtain Pakistan's nuclear weapons. In fact, Allison claims, intelligence reveals that officials of Pakistan's atomic-energy program have met with terrorist leader Osama bin Laden. Second, the tenuous leadership of the current Pakistani regime leaves open the possibility that Islamic factions in Pakistan will gain control of Pakistan's nuclear capabilities. Allison, director of the Belfer Center for Science and International Affairs at Harvard University, is author of Nuclear Terrorism: The Ultimate Preventable Catastrophe.

As you read, consider the following questions:

1. According to Allison, what was Pakistan's response to the story that the founder of its nuclear-weapons program has sold nuclear technology on the black market?

Graham Allison, "Tick, Tick, Tick," *Atlantic Monthly*, October 2004. Reproduced by permission of the author.

2. What has Pakistan done to prevent India from destroying its nuclear arsenal, in the author's opinion?

3. Who might be the unlikely savior of the nuclear dilemma in Pakistan, in the author's view?

Not since the Cuban Missile Crisis of October 1962 have I been as frightened by a single news story as I was by the revelation [in 2003] that Abdul Qadeer Khan, the founder of Pakistan's nuclear-weapons program, had been selling nuclear technology and services on the black market. The story began to break ... after U.S. and British intelligence operatives intercepted a shipment of parts for centrifuges (which are used to enrich uranium for nuclear bombs as well as fuel) on its way from Dubai to Libya. The centrifuges turned out to have been designed by Khan, and before long investigators had uncovered what the head of the International Atomic Energy Agency [IAEA] has called a "Wal-Mart of private-sector proliferation"—a decades-old illicit market in nuclear materials, designs, technologies, and consulting services, all run out of Pakistan.

The Pakistani government's response to the scandal was not reassuring. Khan made a four-minute televised speech on February 4 [2004] asserting that "there was never any kind of authorization for these activities by the government." He took full responsibility for his actions and asked for a pardon, which was immediately granted by President Pervez Musharraf, who essentially buried the affair.... Pakistan's official position remains that no member of Musharraf's government had any concrete knowledge of the illicit transfer—an assertion that U.S. intelligence officials in Pakistan and elsewhere dismiss as absurd. Meanwhile, Pakistani investigators have reportedly questioned a grand total of eleven people from among the country's 6,000 nuclear scientists and 45,000 nuclear workers, and have refused to allow either the United States or the IAEA access to Khan for questioning.

Two Main Threats

Pakistan's nuclear complex poses two main threats. The first—highlighted by Khan's black-market network—is that nuclear weapons, know-how, or materials will find their way into the hands of terrorists. For instance, we have learned that in August of 2001, even as the final planning for [the terrorist attacks of September 11, 2001,] was under way, [terrorist leader] Osama bin Laden received two former officials of Pakistan's atomic-energy program—Sultan Bashiruddin Mahmood and Abdul Majid—at a secret compound near Kabul. Over the course of three days of intense conversation bin Laden and his second-in-command, Ayman al-Zawahiri, grilled Mahmood and Majid about how to make weapons of mass destruction. After Mahmood and Majid were arrested, on October 23, 2001, Mahmood told Pakistani interrogation teams, working in concert with the CIA [Central Intelligence Agency], that Osama bin Laden had expressed a keen interest in nuclear weapons and had sought the scientists' help in recruiting other Pakistani nuclear experts who could provide expertise in the mechanics of bomb-making. CIA Director George Tenet found the report of Mahmood and Majid's meeting with bin Laden so disturbing that he flew directly to Islamabad to confront President Musharraf.

This was not the first time that Pakistani agents had rendered nuclear assistance to dangerous actors: in 1997 Pakistani nuclear scientists made secret trips to North Korea, providing technical support for that country's nuclear-weapons program in exchange for [North Korean capital] Pyongyang's help in developing long-range missiles. And not long ago, according to American intelligence, another Pakistani nuclear scientist negotiated with Libyan agents over the price of nuclear-bomb designs. Pakistan's nuclear program has long been a leaky vessel; the Carnegie Endowment for International Peace has deemed the country "the world's No. 1 nuclear proliferator."

Walking a Razor's Edge

Clearly, there is a significant danger that the black market will put Pakistani nukes (or nuclear material and technical knowledge) in terrorist hands—if it hasn't already. But there is a second, equally significant danger: that a coup might topple Musharraf and leave all or some of Pakistan's nuclear weapons under the control of al-Qaeda, the Taliban, or some other militant Islamic group (or, indeed, under the control of more than one). Part of the problem is that in order to keep its focal enemy, India, from destroying its arsenal in a pre-emptive strike, Pakistan has hidden its nuclear weapons throughout the country; some of them may be in regions that are effectively under fundamentalist Muslim control. Moreover, Pakistan's official alliance with the United States in the war on terror has only increased the danger posed by al-Qaeda sympathizers within its nuclear establishment. Although Musharraf has pledged his "unstinting cooperation in the fight against terrorism," not all the thousands of officers in Pakistan's military and intelligence agencies have signed on. After all, until 9/11 some of them were working closely with members of al-Qaeda and the Taliban. Nor, for that matter, does Pakistan's general population support Musharraf's alliance with the United States. A [March 2004] poll asked Pakistani citizens which leaders in international affairs they viewed favorably. Only seven percent said George W. Bush—and 65 percent said Osama bin Laden.

The uneasy contradiction between Musharraf's pro-American foreign policy and the widespread anti-Americanism within Pakistan has forced Pakistani policymakers to walk a razor's edge. Musharraf faces the clear and present threat of assassination: twice in [2004] he has narrowly escaped attempts on his life. When I spoke to him not long after the second of those attempts, he said he thought he had used up many of his nine lives.

A Record of Proliferation

U.S. policymakers need to be concerned about the Pakistani nuclear arsenal, the level of threat posed to that arsenal by al-Qaeda and related terrorist groups within Pakistan, the stability of Pakistan's regime, and the country's record on nuclear proliferation.

Subodh Atal, Cato Policy Analysis, *March 5, 2003.*

The Role of Islamic Fundamentalists

It may not take a bullet to wrest control over Pakistan's nuclear arsenal from Musharraf. In local elections held in October of 2002 a coalition of fundamentalist parties won command of the government in the North West Frontier Province. The group, known as Muttahida Majlis-e-Amal (MMA), offered a simple platform: pro-Taliban, anti-American, and against all Pakistani involvement in the war on terror. MMA is now the third largest party in Pakistan's parliament; from its new position of strength it has spoken vigorously about the need to regain the honor Pakistan has lost through its subservience to the United States and its struggle with India, with which it has been engaged in a harrowing game of nuclear brinkmanship. To win a vote of confidence that would allow him to serve out his presidential term (which ends in 2007), Musharraf was recently compelled to make a deal with the Islamist parties to step down as head of the military by the end of this year.[1] If all that weren't disconcerting enough, the region the MMA controls happens to be the very one where Osama bin Laden and Ayman al-Zawahiri are currently believed to be hiding.

Under these conditions the emergence of a nuclear-equipped splinter group from within the Pakistani establish-

1. On September 15, 2004, Musharraf for the second time backed down from his commitment to step down as Army Chief and restore democracy, citing national necessity.

ment looks disturbingly plausible. Provoked by anger that Musharraf has made Pakistan a puppet of the United States, such a group would have not only a motive and the domestic political support for a nuclear terrorist act against America but also the organizational competence, the expertise, and the raw material to carry it out.

The Challenge Facing U.S. Policymakers

What to do about this combustible mixture of extreme political instability and nuclear capability is perhaps the most difficult challenge facing U.S. policymakers today. (Consider, for instance, how much simpler it is to deal with North Korea's nuclear program, which is controlled by a monolithic regime and not by layers of governmental subagencies that may have conflicting loyalties and ideologies.) Up to now the [George W.] Bush Administration's response to this challenge has consisted of essentially three ingredients: trying to keep the Pakistani government on America's side in the war on terror (and the Administration deserves credit for carefully nurturing its relationship with Musharraf); examining the possibility of having American forces seize or neutralize Pakistan's nuclear arsenal in an emergency; and blindly hoping that the worst does not occur. But hope, as the well-known saying at the Pentagon goes, is not a plan.

Recent history offers something of a model for how to proceed. In August of 1991 a group of conservatives in the Soviet security establishment attempted to overthrow President Mikhail Gorbachev. Tanks commanded by the coup plotters ringed the Kremlin; Gorbachev, on vacation in the southern part of the country, was placed under house arrest. In the weeks that followed, President George H.W. Bush announced that the United States would unilaterally remove all battlefield nuclear weapons and challenged the Soviet Union to do likewise. The coup was aborted, and Gorbachev responded to Bush's initiative by launching a process that eventually withdrew thousands of Soviet tactical nuclear weapons from the outer reaches of the empire, helping to ensure that the looming dissolution of the Soviet Union would not create more than a dozen new nuclear states. When President Bill Clinton took office, he focused on eliminating the strategic nuclear arsenals that remained in Ukraine, Kazakhstan, and Belarus. By the end of 1996 every one of the nuclear weapons in those states had been deactivated and returned to Russia. Pakistan's situation today is not identical to Russia's in the early 1990s, though the problem of diffused control of nuclear weapons is analogous. But the same lesson applies: it's that alertness in this arena can yield positive results.

Pakistan's Responsibility

Most of what has to be done to secure Pakistan's nuclear weapons and materials will have to be done by the Pakistanis themselves—with American encouragement. One of the more enduring legacies of the Musharraf administration may be the Nuclear Command Authority [NCA], completed in December of 2003. Designed to impose greater centralized control over the Khan Research Laboratories and the Pakistani Atomic Energy Commission, the NCA is headed by Musharraf and vice-chaired by Pakistan's Prime Minister, and is divided into two units—for nuclear weapons and for nuclear scientific personnel—each led by a three-star general.

One option would be for the United States to supply Pakistan with a technology called "permissive action links," which would require Musharraf himself to enter an electronic code before any of the country's nuclear weapons could be deployed. Judging from my conversations with Musharraf . . . , however, the delicacy and sensitivity—and, given the constraints of the nuclear non-proliferation treaty, the legal difficulty—of such a project can hardly be exaggerated. Pakistan's nuclear arsenal is designed first and foremost to deter India. As noted, Pakistan fears that India might locate its nuclear arsenal and destroy its nuclear weapons in a first strike. (Every nuclear power has had similar fears in the early stages of its program.) No reasonable country would divulge information that would leave its arsenal vulnerable to a pre-emptive strike. And even though Pakistan is now an ally of the United States in the war against al-Qaeda, can Musharraf be confident that if the United States provides him with permissive action links, it will not retain some undisclosed ability to disable Pakistan's weapons? An offer of U.S. technical and financial assistance— along with diplomatic assistance in the dispute over Kashmir—might incline Musharraf to let us help him secure electronic control over his arsenal. But we must remember that pushing for too much too soon could destabilize Musharraf—or even lead to his overthrow by someone who is more sympathetic to bin Laden than to the United States.

An Unlikely Savior

Our unlikely savior here might be, of all countries, China. For many years China has acted as an ally, mentor, and supplier of arms to Pakistan, and the two countries are united by their antagonism toward India. If China were to embrace comprehensive security and control of its own arsenal, and be certified by the United States as having done so, then perhaps Musharraf would permit China and the United States each to review the security procedures for half of Pakistan's nuclear weapons and materials, so that neither country could have full knowledge of *all* of Pakistan's arsenal.

The actions required to neutralize the threat of Pakistani proliferation are ambitious; a measure of realism is necessary. But realism need not mean defeatism. In the early 1960s John F. Kennedy predicted that "by 1970 there may be ten nuclear powers instead of four, and by 1975, fifteen or twenty." If those nations with the technical capacity to build nuclear weapons had gone ahead and done so, Kennedy's prediction would have come true. But his warning helped awaken the world to the dangers of unconstrained proliferation. The United States and other nations negotiated international constraints, provided security guarantees, offered inducements, and threatened punishment. Today 187 nations—including scores that have the technical capacity to build nuclear arsenals—have renounced nuclear weapons and committed themselves to the nuclear nonproliferation treaty; only eight states (not the "fifteen or twenty" of Kennedy's prediction) have nuclear weapons. The challenge now is to achieve similar success in blocking the seemingly inexorable path to a nuclear 9/11.

> *"The real threats today are not to be found in actions of North Korea or Iran, but rather in the U.S. . . . self-exemption from international law."*

The United States Is a Dangerous Rogue

Edward Herman

The United States has a history of calling nations rogues so that it can invade them without sanction, maintains Edward Herman in the following viewpoint. In fact, he asserts, the United States meets the very criteria it has established to identify rogue nations. The United States names as rogue those countries that do not abide by international laws, he asserts, yet America reserves the right to flout such laws. The real threat to global security is not Iran or North Korea, he argues, but the United States, a "super-rogue" whose preemptive actions and double standards should be condemned. Herman, an economist and media analyst, is professor emeritus of finance at the University of Pennsylvania.

As you read, consider the following questions:

Edward Herman, "Rogues Have No Right to Self-Defense," *Z Magazine*, August 15, 2003. Reproduced by permission of the author.

1. What examples does Herman provide of the imperial premise that the United States has the right to attack any nation for any reason?

2. According to the author, what nations does the United States exclude from rogue status?

3. Why is the "super-rogue" allowed to continue on its deadly path, in the author's view?

The view that U.S. targets have no right to defend themselves from a U.S. threat or actual attack goes back a long way. During the first three decades of the twentieth century, when the United States was regularly intervening in its backyard to discipline the unruly natives, those who objected and fought against the Marines were always designated "bandits," even when the resistance "was organized, using flags and uniforms" (M. M. Knight, *The Americans in Santo Domingo*).

Denying the Right to Self-Defense

The Vietnamese, in the 1950s and 1960s, resisting a U.S.-imposed puppet ruler and then a direct U.S. invasion, were always terrorists or aggressors in their own country in the U.S. official (and hence media) view, and as Leslie Gelb explained in defending the classification of Vietnam as an "outlaw," they "harmed Americans" who had come to subdue them ([*New York Times*], April 15, 1993).

Gelb, then Foreign Editor of the *New York Times* (and former State Department and Pentagon official), had internalized the imperial premise of a U.S. right to attack and dominate anywhere and for any reason, and the corollary idea that resistance to such actions is criminal.

One of the grotesqueries in U.S. imperialist history has been the regular U.S. practice of threatening some tiny backyard target, preventing its access to weapons from the United States or U.S. allies, and then pointing to the target's acquisition of arms from the Soviet bloc as proof of (1) their aggressive intentions and (2) their links to the larger menace of Soviet aggression.

This was a notable feature of the U.S. direct and proxy attacks on Guatemala in the early 1950s, Cuba from 1959 onward, and Nicaragua in the 1980s. In the case of Nicaragua, U.S. official claims of Soviet MiG fighters on their way to Nicaragua in November 1984—eventually acknowledged to have been straightforward Reagan administration disinformation—caused panic in the media and among leading Democrats, just as a shipment of small arms from Czechoslovakia to Guatemala had done in 1954. These countries had no right to try to defend themselves against ongoing U.S. efforts to overthrow their governments by violence.

Flouting International Law

The premise of the right to attack at imperial discretion implies that international law does not apply to the imperial center, but only to others, and of course the United States has taken this for granted for many decades. For the *New York Times*, "Providence decreed" that we should take over Puerto Rico (1898); for Teddy Roosevelt, U.S. adherence to the Monroe Doctrine "may force the United States, however reluctantly, to the exercise of an international police power" (1904); and for William Howard Taft, the entire hemisphere "will be ours . . . by virtue of our superiority of race" (1912). Modesty has never been a characteristic of U.S. leaders.

The assumption of a right to use force anywhere and unilaterally was prominent in the 2003 invasion of Iraq, but even before the Bush-2 [George W.] era actions involving Iraq, U.S. officials never allowed international law to interfere with policy.

For example, in the Reagan years the International Court finding that the United States had engaged in "unlawful acts" and owed Nicaragua reparations was simply ignored, and the administration vetoed a [United Nations (UN)] Security Council resolution calling upon all countries to abide by international law! During Bush-1's [George H.W.'s]tenure the United States not only vetoed a Security Council condemnation of the U.S. invasion of Panama, it maneuvered the UN into sanctioning a war against Iraq by fending off all negotiating efforts, and conducted that war in violation of numerous international prohibitions (e.g., [by using] cluster bombs, fuel air explosives, depleted uranium, burying large numbers of Iraqi soldiers in bulldozed sand, and deliberately destroying Iraq's water supply facilities).

[Former president Bill] Clinton carried on this great tradition, in the case of Iraq, aggressively implementing the sanctions policy of deliberate deprivation of medicines and means of repairing the water system destroyed in 1991, with enormous civilian casualties, in clear violation of international law as regards the treatment of civilian populations. The "no-fly zones" in Iraq were not authorized by any UN resolution and the destruction and scores of civilian deaths resulting from U.S.-British air attacks on Iraq during the dozen years before the 2003 invasion were therefore criminal acts.

As with the Vietnamese daring to shoot at U.S. soldiers invading their country, so Iraqi missiles aimed at U.S. and British aircraft prior to the March 18–19, 2003 invasion represent unjustified "attacks" that "demonstrate Iraq's contempt for UN resolutions" according to [U.S. secretary of defense] Donald Rumsfeld (BBC [British Broadcasting Corporation], "Iraq intensifies 'attacks,' says US," Sept. 30, 2002). Iraq, like all other U.S. targets, has never had any right of self-defense.

The Right to Name Rogues

The United States also takes upon itself the right to name rogues, as it has long done terrorist organizations and terror states. Naturally, as super-rogue, it does not name itself, despite its unsurpassed rogue credentials. . . .

Cartoon by Kirk Anderson. Reproduced by permission of Kirk Anderson.

It also excludes its allies and clients, just as it denies them terror-state status, no matter how excellent their qualifications. It is easy to see why the super-rogue has decided that it will oppose, possibly by force, any other country developing the capacity to challenge its military hegemony: this permits the super-rogue to behave like a rogue itself while self-righteously naming (and attacking) targets (i.e., alleged "rogues") of choice.

Super-Rogue Behavior

Super-rogue behavior has been dramatically evident in the Iraq sanctions, invasion and occupation. Super-rogue was able to impose punitive sanctions on Iraq that involved treating 23 million civilians as hostages to the demand for regime change for twelve years, in the process killing over a million of those civilians.

This was done with the cooperation of [Secretary-General] Kofi Annan and the UN, and with no outcry or protest from the "international community," media or "cruise missile left."[1] Super-rogue was then able to invade and occupy Iraq in blatant violation of the UN Charter, after having made fools of the inspectors and UN, and he did this without the slightest penalty from the same "international community" that had punished Vietnam severely for invading Cambodia and overthrowing Pol Pot, an invasion that took place only after repeated attacks on Vietnam by Pol Pot's forces. Iraq of course had not attacked the United States or Britain and had no capability of doing so. In short, UN sanctions have nothing to do with principles; they only follow demands and/or approval of the principal (super-rogue).

It is now generally acknowledged, even by some U.S. officials, that the attack on Iraq was based on serial lies concerning Iraq's weapons of mass destruction (WMD) and the threat that they posed to U.S. and British national security. It is also evident that the U.S. attack on Iraq once again involved the use of anti-civilian weapons (cluster bombs, depleted uranium), deliberate attacks on many sites where civilians were likely to be killed, and over 5,000 civilian deaths.

It is also evident that the U.S. government has violated the obligation of an occupying army to provide security and assure basic services to the civilian population of the occupied territory; that it came in prepared only to protect the oil ministry and oil resources; and that it has given highest priority to hunting for Saddam Hussein rather than assuring even minimal services to the victimized population.

The Reaction of
the International Community

But despite the illegality-plus-lie basis of the conquest, and the gross mishandling and illegalities of the occupation, and

1. Commentators who, according to Herman, claim to speak from the left but who have aligned themselves with the national leadership to support aggressive military interventionism and projection of power abroad. Herman contends that they are not the genuine left—those who oppose the powerful in the interest of the non-elite majority.

the obvious intent to rule Iraq directly or via proxies, the international community has not called for punishing the killers of over 5,000 civilians (plus innumerable other crimes) and forcing the aggressors-murderers out. Three thousand dead U.S. citizens on 9/11 was unbearable in the United States and aroused the deepest sympathy and understanding on the part of the "international community," for whom it justified a vengeance assault on Afghanistan and declaration of a global "war on terror."

But 5,000+ Iraqi civilians killed on the basis of lies is quite bearable, and the New Hitler will not even be deprived of the fruits of his conquest, let alone be subjected to sanctions. He is merely urged to farm out some of the management responsibilities to the UN and to move more rapidly to that democratic state that he belatedly claimed to be his objective in regime change in Iraq. But there are no threats or penalties for misbehavior, which is why super-rogue finds it so satisfying to be super-rogue and promises to use force to assure preservation of his super-rogue status.

Setting the Agenda

And super-rogue can continue to set the agenda on "threats" for the UN and international community. The world's people may, despite control of the global media by friends of super-rogue, believe that super-rogue himself, with his invasions of Afghanistan and Iraq, his continuing military buildup and drumbeat of threats to use force unilaterally, his open-ended "war on terror" being carried out in cooperation with junior-partner rogues like [Israeli prime minister Ariel] Sharon, constitutes far and away the world's greatest threat to peace, security, and even survival.

But super-rogue says that North Korea's and Iran's quest for nuclear weapons is a very very serious problem that amounts to "crises," and news reports tell of well-developed U.S. plans to attack these rogues and put a stop to their nefarious behavior. The Western media and even the liberals swallow this, agreeing that these are crises and major threats, with the debate over whether we can solve this problem by negotiations (the liberals) or must go in and "take out" the threatening weapons and/or regimes.

One pathetic liberal gambit has been to criticize the Bush cabal's focus on Iraq, which doesn't have a bomb, while neglecting the fearsome threat that North Korea in the meantime might be acquiring a nuclear weapon. This inflates the threat of North Korea's possible possession of a nuclear weapon, which it could not use without committing national suicide. It ignores the fact that North Korea and Iran are compelled to seek such weapons because the United States openly threatens to use such weapons against them.

It ignores the fact that Israel has been allowed—even helped—to acquire a nuclear weapons arsenal without penalty, and is permitted by super-rogue and the international community to do so, while countries threatened by Israel's weaponry cannot do the same without constituting a "threat." It ignores the fact that the super-rogue is the only country that has used nuclear weapons and now threatens their further use even more openly.

The Real Threat

In short, the real threats today are not to be found in actions of North Korea or Iran, but rather in the U.S. rejection of the Non-Proliferation Treaty promise to refrain from the use of nuclear weapons against non-nuclear states; its threat to use these and its other weapons in "preemptive" (in reality, preventive) actions against targets of choice; its self-exemption from international law; and its double standard support for Israel's freedom to acquire nuclear weapons while such efforts by Israel's opponents are intolerable.

The response of the UN and international community to these real threats has been in the same pattern as their treatment of the U.S. plan to attack Iraq. That is, instead of opposing the U.S. threats and plans of aggression against its targets, the UN and international community accept the U.S. premises that its targets pose the threat. And just as they rushed to accommodate the super-rogue with intensified inspections to deal with that monstrous threat of Iraq's WMD, they now rush to persuade North Korea and Iran to be reasonable, accept international inspections, and give up any desire they might have to acquire nuclear arms.

Once again those threatened by the super-rogue are not granted the right to defend themselves, not only by super-rogue but by the UN and "international community." But this failure to contest super-rogue's actions and policies encourages him to continue on his deadly path, and it will hardly deter his prospective victims from seeking to protect themselves.

Periodical Bibliography

The following articles have been selected to supplement the diverse views presented in this chapter.

Reza Aslan — "Misunderstanding Iran," *Nation*, February 28, 2005.

Subodh Atal — "Extremist, Nuclear Pakistan: An Emerging Threat?" *Cato Policy Analysis*, March 5, 2003.

Doug Bandow — "Bring the Troops Home: Ending the Obsolete Korean Commitment," *Cato Policy Analysis*, May 7, 2003.

Banning N. Garrett and Dennis M. Sherman — "Non-globalized States Pose a Threat," *Yale Global*, July 7, 2003. http://yaleglobal.yale.edu/display.article?id=2032.

Selig S. Harrison — "The North Korean Conundrum," *Nation*, June 7, 2004.

John Keegan — "We Should Be Very Worried About Iran," *London Daily Telegraph*, January 12, 2006.

Daniel Kennelly et al. — "Our Dangerous Muddle in North Korea," *American Enterprise*, July/August 2005.

Michael Ledeen — "Syrious Threat," *National Review*, March 11, 2005.

Kongdan Oh and Ralph C. Hassig — "North Korea's Nuclear Politics," *Current History*, September 2004.

Bill Powell et al. — "The Man Who Sold the Bomb," *Time*, February 14, 2005.

John M. Swomley — "The Ultimate Rogue Nation," *Humanist*, January 1, 2001.

Ray Takeyh — "Iran's Nuclear Calculations," *World Policy Journal*, Summer 2003.

CHAPTER 2

What Threats Do Rogue Nations Pose?

Chapter Preface

On July 9, 1962, the U.S. military launched a Thor missile carrying a 1.4-megaton warhead from Johnston Island in the Pacific Ocean. The warhead was detonated at an altitude of 250 miles. Street lamps on the island of Oahu went dark, and telephone service on Kauai was disrupted. Cecil Coale, an electrical engineer tasked with monitoring the detonation on a magnetometer, describes the experience:

> A brilliant white flash erased the darkness like a photoflash. Then the entire sky turned light green for about a second. In several more seconds, a deep red aurora, several moon diameters in size, formed where the blast had been. . . . The strip chart recorders hummed loudly. . . . Wow, was there a big change in the Earth's magnetic field! Welcome to the electromagnetic pulse!

This test revealed a new kind of nuclear attack—the electromagnetic pulse (EMP).

Some security analysts worry that rogue nations that might not have the ability to launch a direct, long-range nuclear attack could instead launch an EMP attack by attaching a nuclear weapon to a Scud missile. The Scud missile, a tactical Russian ballistic missile exported widely to other countries, could then be launched from an offshore freighter to detonate over a target. An EMP attack could knock out power grids and other electrical systems for months or even years, some experts claim. According to U.S. Senator Jon Kyl, "Communication would be largely impossible. Lack of refrigeration would leave food rotting in warehouses, exacerbated by a lack of transportation, as those vehicles still working simply ran out of gas (which is pumped with electricity). The inability to sanitize and distribute water would quickly threaten public health." As is true in natural or other disasters, asserts Kyl, "such circumstances often result in a fairly rapid breakdown of social order." Such an attack, these analysts assert, poses a serious threat to international security. Other commentators contend, however, that such claims are exaggerated, designed to frighten American citizens into supporting missile defense programs.

Some experts believe that an EMP attack launched by a rogue nation is likely. U.S. intelligence indicates that several rogue nations have the technological capacity to detonate a nuclear warhead in the atmosphere using a Scud missile. Iran, for example, has conducted midflight missile detonations. More worrisome, some analysts assert, are intelligence reports that rogue North Korea is exporting missile technology to terrorists and other rogue nations. "Scuds can easily be purchased on the open market for about $100,000 apiece," says Kyl. Rogue nations that have Scud missiles and nuclear warheads, these analysts argue, could easily launch an EMP attack.

Other analysts contend that the EMP threat has been exaggerated to gain support for the Bush administration's missile defense program. Philip Coyle, former assistant secretary of defense and Pentagon director of operational test and evaluation during the Bill Clinton administration, contends that an EMP attack by a rogue nation is unlikely. He argues that the EMP Commission, created to evaluate the EMP threat, made "calculations of extreme weapons effects as if they were a proven fact, and further [puffed up] rogue nations and terrorists with the capabilities of giants." Physicist Richard Garwin agrees: "People who argue for missile defense use the most bizarre arguments." He claims that even nations with advanced nuclear arms, no less rogue nations and terrorists, would confront significant technological hurdles in launching an EMP attack.

Whether rogue nations could completely disrupt the U.S. economy and threaten public health with an EMP attack or whether such claims are exaggerated to promote U.S. missile defense programs remains controversial. The authors in the following chapter express their views on other threats posed by rogue nations.

> "We face significant challenges from terrorist-sponsoring regimes that are developing weapons of mass destruction in many forms."

Rogue Nations Pose a Serious Nuclear Threat

John R. Bolton

Rogue nations that pursue nuclear weapons in violation of the Non-Proliferation Treaty (NPT) threaten global security, argues John R. Bolton in the following viewpoint. Iran, he asserts, continues to deceive the International Atomic Energy Agency about the true purpose of its nuclear program. Ostensibly pursued in order to produce nuclear power, it is in reality a covert nuclear weapons program. North Korea is also developing nuclear weapons and might sell nuclear materials and arms to terrorists, Bolton maintains. Bolton, who at the time of this statement was undersecretary of defense for arms control and international security, is currently U.S. ambassador to the United Nations.

Editor's Note: The following viewpoint is from a speech presented by Bolton at the third Preparatory Meeting of the Non-Proliferation Treaty Review Conference in New York City.

John R. Bolton, "The NPT: A Crisis of Non-Compliance" Statement to the Third Session of the Preparatory Committee for the 2005 Review Conference of the Treaty on the Non-Proliferation of Nuclear Weapons, U.S. Department of State, Washington, DC.

As you read, consider the following questions:

1. According to Bolton, Iran has failed to disclose or explain the exploration of what technologies?

2. In the author's opinion, what is suspect about Iran's ambitious reactor program?

3. What should other countries learn from Libya's commitment to end its WMD programs, according to Qadaffi, as cited by Bolton?

The United States supports the Non-Proliferation Treaty [NPT] and is committed to its goals. But despite our strong support, the support of many NPT countries and the best intentions of most of you here [at the third Preparatory Meeting of the Non-Proliferation Treaty Review Conference], at least four NPT non-nuclear member countries were or are using the NPT as cover for the development of nuclear weapons. States like Iran are actively violating their treaty obligations, and have gained access to technologies and materials for their nuclear weapons programs. North Korea violated its NPT obligations while a party, and then proved its strategic decision to seek nuclear weapons by withdrawing from the Treaty entirely. Two states in the past—Iraq and Libya—had also violated the NPT. Libya took the important decision to disclose and eliminate its weapons of mass destruction [WMD] programs, a paradigm that other nations now seeking nuclear weapons should emulate.

There is a crisis of NPT noncompliance, and the challenge before us is to devise ways to ensure full compliance with the Treaty's nonproliferation objectives. Without such compliance by all members, confidence in the security benefits derived from the NPT will erode. To address this serious problem, President [George W.] Bush ... announced a series of proposals that are aimed at strengthening compliance with the obligations we all undertook when we signed the Treaty. These proposals will address a fundamental problem that has allowed nations like Iran and North Korea to exploit the benefits of NPT membership to develop their nuclear weapons programs. The President is determined to stop rogue states from gaining nuclear weapons under cover of supposed peaceful nuclear technology. As President Bush said on February 11, [2004,] "Proliferators must not be allowed to cynically manipulate the NPT to acquire the material and infrastructure necessary for manufacturing illegal weapons." . . .

The Challenge of Iran

We face significant challenges from terrorist-sponsoring regimes that are developing weapons of mass destruction in many forms. Today, I would like to focus on three very different cases, one a major success story for nonproliferation, and two where the nuclear proliferation threat to international peace and security continues to grow.

First, Iran, one of the most fundamental challenges to the non-proliferation regime, which has concealed a large-scale covert nuclear weapons program for over eighteen years. It is clear that Iran draws from many of the same networks that supplied Libya with nuclear technology, components, and materials, including the A.Q. Khan [the father of Pakistan's nuclear weapons program] network, as Khan himself has confessed.

It is no surprise that the IAEA [International Atomic Energy Agency] has uncovered much evidence of Iran's undeclared activity. There is as yet, however, no reason to believe that Iran has made a strategic decision to abandon its nuclear weapons program and its violation of its NPT Article II obligations. Iran's recent failures to disclose work on uranium enrichment centrifuges of an advanced design and on Polonium-210, and to explain the presence of highly enriched uranium, are clear indicators that Iran continues its quest for nuclear weapons. Following an all-too-familiar pattern, Iran omitted this information from its October 2003 declaration to the

A New and Dangerous Era

If North Korea and Iran are allowed to build and hold nuclear weapons, other countries are likely to follow, making the world much more dangerous. We may, in fact, be on the leading edge of a new era in which more and more countries race to get nuclear weapons—which are a lot easier to design, build, and hide than they were years ago.

David E. Sanger, New York Times Upfront, *January 24, 2005.*

IAEA—a declaration that Iran said provided the "full scope of Iranian nuclear activities" and a "complete centrifuge R&D [research & development] chronology."

A Pattern of Deception

Iran has expressed interest in the purchase of up to six additional nuclear power plants, and has told the IAEA that it is pursuing a heavy-water research reactor at Arak—a type of reactor that might be well suited for plutonium production. This ambitious reactor program is a remarkable venture for a country whose oil and gas reserves will last several hundred years. There is no conceivable economic justification for Iran to build costly nuclear fuel cycle facilities to support a small "nuclear power" program. It is clear that the primary role of Iran's "nuclear power" program is to serve as a cover and a pretext for the import of nuclear technology and expertise that can be used to support nuclear weapons development.

Iran's continued deception and delaying tactics have not gone unnoticed by the international community. Despite Iran's massive deception and denial campaign, the IAEA has uncovered a large amount of information indicating numerous major violations of Iran's treaty obligations under its NPT Safeguards Agreement. On the basis of the evidence collected by

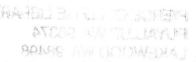

IAEA inspectors and exhaustively documented in his reports, the Director General [of the IAEA] has concluded that, "it is clear that Iran has failed in a number of instances over an extended period of time to meet its obligations under its Safeguards Agreement. . . ."

Answering Unresolved Questions

The IAEA Statute requires that the IAEA Board of Governors report non-compliance with safeguards obligations to the United Nations Security Council. In the U.S. view, this standard was clearly met as early as June [2003]. Iranian noncompliance with safeguards obligations has been manifest for many months, and both the Board and the Director General have noted Iran's multiple breaches and failures in this regard. We did not press for such a report at the March [2004] meeting. The IAEA Board will at some point, however, need to fulfill its responsibility under the IAEA Statute to report the safeguards failures found in Iran to the Security Council, as it did in the case of Libya. If Iran continues its unwillingness to comply with the NPT, the Council can then take up this issue as a threat to international peace and security. If the Council is unable to do so, it will not only be a blow to our efforts to hold Iran accountable, but also a blow to the effectiveness of the Council itself and to the credibility of the entire NPT regime.

Iran's oil rich environment, grudging cooperation with the IAEA, its deception, and its 18 year record of clandestine activity leads us to the inevitable conclusion that Iran is lying and that its goal is to develop a nuclear weapon in violation of its Article II commitments. We believe that Iran's stalling tactics clearly indicate that it has not fulfilled even the minimal steps it agreed to last September [2003] and again in February [2004]. If we permit Iran's deception to go on much longer, it will be too late. Iran will have nuclear weapons.

If Iran wants to restore international confidence in its civilian nuclear program, it must "come clean" and answer satisfactorily all unresolved IAEA questions. Iran must make a clear decision to open up its nuclear program to transparent inspections, including full access under the Additional Protocol, and comply with all of its NPT and IAEA responsibilities. If Iran does not do this, it will remain in violation of Article II of the Treaty and, according to Article IV, will forfeit any right to civilian nuclear power assistance.

The Ambitions of North Korea

North Korea's use of the NPT as a cover to hide its nuclear weapons ambitions and its subsequent withdrawal from the Treaty constitute the clearest example of a state cynically manipulating the NPT to threaten the international community with its nuclear weapons program. We now face the danger not only of a North Korea in possession of nuclear weapons, but the risk that it will export fissile material or weapons to other rogue states or to terrorists. Continuous international pressure is essential to ensure the complete, verifiable, and irreversible dismantlement of its nuclear weapons program, including both its plutonium and uranium enrichment programs. The United States continues to support the Six-Party Process,[1] but we have long said that we will measure success in the talks through concrete progress. Simply continuing to talk, however, is not progress. And as Vice President [Dick] Cheney ... stated in China, "Time is not necessarily on our side." We urge all member states to support the Six-Party talks aimed at achieving a peaceful, diplomatic end to North Korea's nuclear programs.

---

1. The Six-Party Process was a series of talks between the governments of six countries—Japan, Russia, the United States, China, and North and South Korea—beginning in 2003 to discuss North Korea's development of a nuclear program.

Success in Libya

On December 19, 2003, Libya announced that it would voluntarily rid itself of its WMD equipment and programs. Libya declared its intention to comply in full with the NPT and to sign the Additional Protocol. All of these remarkable steps, Libya announced, would be undertaken "in a transparent way that could be proved, including accepting immediate international inspection."

Libya has made enormous progress toward fulfilling these commitments. In cooperation with the United States, the United Kingdom, and the IAEA, Libya has dismantled its known nuclear weapons program. In cooperation with the United Kingdom, Libya and the IAEA, we removed nuclear weapon design documents, gas centrifuge components designed to enrich uranium, containers of uranium hexafluoride (UF6), a uranium conversion facility, and 15 kilograms of fresh high-enriched uranium reactor fuel which was removed to Russia.

As Colonel [Muammar] Qadaffi said . . . in his speech to the Organization of African Unity, "The security of Libya does not come from the nuclear bomb, the nuclear bomb represents a danger to the country which has them." If they wish to rejoin the community of civilized nations, states like Iran and North Korea could learn from Libya's recent example. On December 19, 2003, when Libya made its WMD commitment, the President of the United States indicated that fulfillment of Libya's commitment would open the way for better relations with the United States. We meant exactly that. . . . The President decided to terminate application of the Iran and Libya Sanctions Act ("ILSA") on Libya. The President is changing the Executive Order sanctions under the International Emergency Economic Powers Act that will enable trade with Libya. The United States will not be the only nation that seeks to improve its relations with Libya, but based upon changed behavior by the Libyan regime, we believe that these steps toward better relations are warranted. As President Bush said in February [2004], "Abandoning the pursuit of illegal weapons can lead to better relations with the United States, and other free nations. Continuing to seek those weapons will not bring security or international prestige, but only political isolation, economic hardship, and other unwelcome consequences."

As I said at the outset, the United States is committed to a strong and effective nuclear non-proliferation regime. But the time for business as usual is over. An irresponsible handful of nations not living up to their Treaty commitments are undermining the NPT's mission. Without full compliance by all NPT members, confidence in the NPT as a nonproliferation instrument erodes. What will eventually result is a world with an ever-growing number of states possessing nuclear weapons, where terrorists and rogue states would have expanded access to nuclear technology and expertise. In such a world, the risk of catastrophic attacks against civilized nations would be far greater.

> *"The reluctance of the major Western democracies to destroy their own nuclear stockpiles [does not] do much to persuade others to steer clear of atomic weapons."*

The Rogue Nuclear Threat Is a Reaction to Western Aggression

Mario Basini

The quest to develop nuclear weapons by so-called rogue nations is a reaction to the aggression and hypocrisy of the Western nuclear powers, claims Mario Basini in the following viewpoint. At the same time that Western powers condemn the nuclear aspirations of nations unfriendly to the West, they refuse to reduce their own nuclear stockpiles, he argues. Moreover, Basini maintains, nations seek nuclear arms in order to protect themselves from the aggression of nuclear states such as Great Britain and the United States. Basini is a staff writer for the Western Mail, *a Welsh newspaper.*

As you read, consider the following questions:

Mario Basini, "Why We Should Disarm Before Expecting the Same of Others," *Western Mail (Cardiff, UK)*, May 14, 2005. Reproduced by permission.

1. In Basini's view, why do President Bush and Prime Minister Blair condemn the nuclear aspirations of some countries but not others?

2. According to the author, what was clear even before the invasion of Iraq exploded the myth of Iraq's stockpiles of weapons?

3. What kind of research is the United States continuing to pursue, in the author's opinion?

If you were born within the shadow of World War Two, a [May 2005] conference in New York ... could revive your worst nightmare. The phrases 'mushroom cloud', 'nuclear holocaust' and 'atomic winter' may have the old-fashioned ring of an Aldermaston March.[1] But just two decades ago they conjured up the very real threat of a devastation so great it would end our civilisation.

The two superpowers, the United States and the Soviet Union, had arsenals of nuclear weapons trained on each other which were so vast they could have destroyed the planet several times over. Every time they squared up to each other—over the Cuban Missile Crisis, for example, or the Korean War—the rest of us felt our time had come.

The demise of the Soviet Union should have put an end to all that. The newly-democratic Russia still has a formidable nuclear stockpile, but it is now officially a friend. The nuclear arms race is well and truly over. Or is it?

A New Threat

The confrontation of two implacably hostile governments has been replaced by a proliferation of smaller nuclear powers each of which could yet trigger a holocaust through the use oits own nuclear weapons. Add to that the problem of the black market trade in bombs and weapons-grade uranium and you have a picture of a world facing a greater nuclear threat than ever before.

1. A 1958 anti–nuclear weapons march from London to Aldermaston, the location of a British nuclear weapons facility.

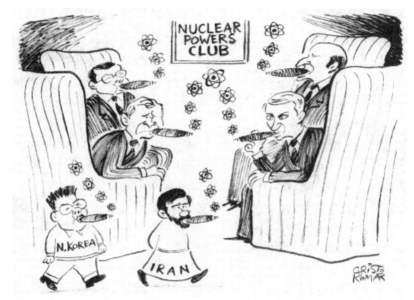

Cartoon by Christo Komarnitski. Reproduced by permission of PoliticalCartoons.com.

Which is why that conference in New York, lasting most of [May 2005], is still so crucial to our future. It is a regular five-year review of the Nuclear Non-Proliferation Treaty—NPT for short—which has attempted to control the number of nuclear weapons in the world since 1970.

The disapproval of the major nuclear countries—The United States, Britain, France, Russia and China—has fallen most heavily on those 'rogue states', which may not be developing nuclear weapons merely for their self-defence. They may also be prepared to arm any terrorists they sponsor. High on this list are, of course, two members of the United States' 'axis of evil'—Iran and North Korea.

As a BBC [British Broadcasting Corporation] investigation showed [in May 2005], Iran appears extremely reluctant to allow UN [United Nations] inspectors to take a hard look at its nuclear programme supposedly dedicated to the peaceful production of electricity. North Korea has refused to even sign up to the NPT.

A Treaty's Failure

The treaty and its main sponsor, the US, are obviously failing to deter smaller powers from successfully acquiring nuclear weapons. Among the reasons for that are the attitudes of the major Western democracies to their own nuclear arsenals and to some rogue states.

The condemnation of President [George W.] Bush and [British prime minister Tony] Blair of nuclear weapon-possessing countries with different ideologies like Iran and North Korea is unequivocal. They are much more reluctant to condemn friendly states which have developed nuclear armaments. Israel, for example, has indicated it would not hesitate to use its own nuclear missiles if it felt its existence was threatened. India and Pakistan, both allies of Britain and the United States, may yet trigger a major nuclear war by attacking each other.

One reason why the NPT has so far proved ineffective in preventing the growth of nuclear weapons lies in the treaty itself.

As a carrot for not developing nuclear bombs, the major powers promised to provide small states with 'atoms for peace'. They would supply the technology needed to develop peaceful atomic energy, provided the recipients steered clear of bombs.

The problem is that the technology needed to produce electricity in nuclear power stations is very similar to that needed for nuclear weapons. Once, for example, a country has the means of enriching uranium for peaceful purposes, it is well on the way to making the fuel it needs to produce bombs.

A Reaction to Western Aggression

Ironically, the Iraqi invasion [of 2003], designed to remove a major 'rogue state' from the world map, may have encouraged others to defy Britain and the US and produce nuclear armaments of their own. Even before the invasion exploded the myth of Iraq's stockpiles of chemical and biological weapons, it was obvious that [Iraqi leader] Saddam Hussein did not possess nuclear weapons. If he had, say the critics, America and Britain would never have dared invade for fear of retaliation.

The message that has been sent to smaller countries is that if you want to protect yourself from invasion you had better develop your own nuclear bomb. Witness the way Bush and Blair refuse to contemplate attacks on Iran or North Korea.

Nor does the reluctance of the major Western democracies to destroy their own nuclear stockpiles do much to persuade others to steer clear of atomic weapons. Under the terms of the NPT the United States may have drastically reduced the number of its weapons. But it still has 4,900 warheads on missiles able to be delivered from bombers or submarines.

Even as it is urging smaller countries not to develop nuclear armaments, the United States continues its research into the production of more advanced, more precisely targeted weapons. Now we learn that Britain, too, could be about to update its Trident missile system at massive cost.

Helping to strengthen and update the Nuclear Nonproliferation Treaty may be an important step towards freeing the world from the threat of nuclear terror. But until major democracies like Britain and America end their hypocritical stance on their own arsenals and on those of states they regard as allies, the destruction of the planet in a nuclear war remains a distinct possibility.

"State support of terrorist organizations [is] among the primary reasons that terrorism now commands a central role in international relations."

Rogue Nations Support Terrorism

Yoram Schweitzer

Rogue nations' support of terrorists helps spread terrorism, claims Yoram Schweitzer in the following viewpoint. He cites, for example, Libya's notorious support of terrorists. For decades Libyan leader Muammar Qadaffi used terrorism to call international attention to his regime, assassinate exiles, and retaliate against the United States and Great Britain when they tried to restrain his murderous campaign, argues Schweitzer. Only when Libya was held responsible for terrorist acts and subjected to sanctions did the nation break its terrorist connections, he asserts. Schweitzer is a research associate with the Jaffee Center for Strategic Studies in Tel Aviv, Israel.

As you read, consider the following questions:

1. In Schweitzer's view, how does the media portrayal contrast with the real reasons that Libya changed its policy toward terrorism?

Yoram Schweitzer, "Neutralizing Terrorism-Sponsoring States: The Libyan Model," *Strategic Assessment*, May 7, 2004. Reproduced by permission.

2. What does the author claim is the main challenge in compelling states to abandon their terrorism-sponsoring policies?

3. According to the author, what processes were unfolding in the international arena that provided a backdrop to the international coalition against Libya?

Over the past few months [of spring 2004], Libya has taken final steps to return to the community of law-abiding nations and to the arena of consensus within the international community. Libya's actions follow decades of being cast as a pariah state, primarily due to its support of international terrorism and its involvement in developing non-conventional weapons. Such an extreme and seemingly sudden reversal in the foreign policy of a "rogue" state is not a routine development in international relations. Perhaps for this reason it is a particularly encouraging indication of the possibility of putting rogue states back on the "normative" track without the use of military force, but rather by means of diplomatic activity complemented by sanctions enforced and coordinated by many countries, especially ones with international political and economic influence.

In contrast to its portrayal in the media, the change in Libyan policy was gradual and protracted. The neutralization of Libya as a terrorism-sponsoring state was a process that lasted years and involved a combination of political and economic sanctions that cost Libya more than $30 billion in economic damage. Yet the geopolitical implications of [the terrorist attacks of] September 11, 2001 and the military action undertaken against individual rogue states by the American-led international anti-terrorism coalition are what appear to have convinced Libyan ruler Muammar Qaddafi to accelerate the process of terminating his membership in the community of disreputable rogue states and ceasing his country's development of non-conventional weapons. . . .

State Involvement in Terrorism

The history of international terrorism over the past four decades reveals that state involvement in terrorism and state support of terrorist organizations are among the primary reasons that terrorism now commands a central role in international relations. Terrorism emerges from many varied root causes and is exercised by perpetrators who act in the name of a range of ideologies in different geographical areas. On the whole, it is safe to assume that terrorism would exist even without the assistance of sovereign states. Still, without states' active and passive support of terrorism, be it direct or indirect, terrorist organizations would not possess the impressive capabilities to survive and inflict damage, powers that lend them the ability to influence international political affairs so significantly.

The main challenge in compelling states to abandon a terrorism-sponsoring policy stems from the difficulty of acquiring legal proof of their involvement in terrorism, because countries do not claim responsibility for terrorist attacks in which they are directly or indirectly involved. When they are accused of involvement, they cling to a policy of denial. As a result, terrorism-sponsoring states are able to continue working behind the scenes and use terrorism to advance their interests. Instances in which states have been caught redhanded—where it has been possible to prove their guilt publicly in a court of law without having to endanger sensitive intelligence sources—are rare.

The Impact of Multi-national Sanctions

Aside from the experience of Libya, two additional cases are worth mentioning in which rogue states were deterred from continuing their intensive and direct involvement in international terrorist attacks: Syria and Iran. A change in policy of these two countries was less dramatic than with Libya, and only occurred after their involvement in terrorism was ex-

State Accomplices to Terrorist Crimes

The states that choose to harbor terrorists are like accomplices who provide shelter for criminals. They will be held accountable for their "guests'" actions. International terrorists should know, before they contemplate a crime, that they cannot hunker down in safehaven for a period of time and be absolved of their crimes.

Office of the Coordinator for Counterterrorism,
"Patterns of Global Terrorism 2000," April 30, 2001.

posed in public court rulings that pointed to senior officials' direct responsibility for attacks that were planned or executed in Europe. . . . The different international responses to these states, however, as opposed to the response to Libyan involvement in terrorism, were at least in part a function of casualty results. In the Syrian instance, the attack on [an] El Al plane was foiled and therefore resulted in no casualties, while in the Iranian instance the number of people killed in Germany—in this case Kurdish exiles—was relatively small. [This incident] thus represented another example of German government and European tolerance towards rogue states settling their own domestic scores on European soil. The sanctions that Europe and the United States applied against these two countries were circumscribed in scope and in time, and therefore they proved of limited though nonetheless important influence. Syria and Iran were successfully deterred from further overt, direct involvement in international terrorism.

An important inference that emerges from these events is that a coordinated multi-national policy that sets a high enough price tag for any country that is proven guilty in a court of law is likely to cause a terrorism-sponsoring state to seriously reconsider the cost-effectiveness of its policy. Therefore, we can conclude that there is a need to design a global policy, involving as many countries as possible, that raises the cost to terrorism-sponsoring states to one that will outweigh the potential benefits and deter them from even indirect or passive involvement in terrorism.

The Libyan Example

Libya's distancing from international terrorism began more than a decade ago. As Libya was undoubtedly one of the states most actively involved in international terrorism for twenty years, its neutralization as a state supporter of terrorism was a critical factor in the disappearance of a number of dominant international terrorist organizations.

Under the regime established by Colonel Muammar Qaddafi at the end of the 1960s, Libya embraced terrorism as a tool to fortify the regime and disseminate its revolutionary ideology. Qaddafi used terrorism on a number of different levels, acquiring for himself and his regime an international reputation of revolutionary. Libya, which had previously been a country of peripheral importance in terms of international relations, became the object of an unusual degree of international interest in the 1970s and 1980s due to the country's power and importance in terms of "geo-terrorism." Qaddafi exercised state terror against opponents of his regime within Libya itself and cruelly crushed every attempt to remove him from power. By means of intelligence agents who operated in Arab and Western countries, he resorted to terrorism against exiles and opponents living outside of Libya and assassinated dozens of opponents of the regime with complete disregard for the laws of the host countries. . . .

The Gradual Turnaround

Two decades of hindsight allow us to determine that the turnaround in Libya's involvement in international terrorism stemmed, ironically, from the escalation in the use of terrorism against the West. Recourse to terrorist attacks that were especially bloody, even for a state that had previously not been shy of violent means to achieve political ends, is what eventually led Libya to its entanglement, exposure, and punishment.

Libya's direct involvement in international terrorism peaked in the mid-1980s, and Qaddafi did not go to great lengths to deny it, at least not on ideological grounds. In the wake of a series of terrorist attacks in late 1985 by Abu Nidal's group that resulted in the death of American citizens, the United States, which led the campaign against international terrorism, took countermeasures. . . .

Despite the impression imprinted on public memory that Qaddafi was deterred by America's display of strength in [the Libyan capital,] Tripoli, the Libyan leader actually responded to the American attack with a murderous campaign of terrorist attacks through the Abu Nidal Organization and the Japanese Red Army. Serving as proxy organizations for Libya, these groups attacked American and British targets in Pakistan, Italy, India, Sudan, and Indonesia. Qaddafi's counterattack reached a new height on December 21, 1988, when at his direction Libyan agents blew up Pan American flight 103 above Lockerbie, Scotland, killing 270 people. The following September, Qaddafi proteges assisted the cell responsible for blowing up a plane of the French airline UTA in the skies above Niger, resulting in the death of 169 passengers and crew.

A joint American-British investigatory commission, which published its findings in November 1991, pointed to Libya as the party directly responsible for the explosion aboard the Pan Am flight and the mass killing of citizens of various nationalities. Exposure of Libya's involvement in the explosion aboard the French plane facilitated the consolidation of a broad and coordinated international coalition which, for the first time in the history of the international struggle against modern terrorism, succeeded in imposing and enforcing effective sanctions against a terrorism-sponsoring state under the auspices of the United Nations Security Council. . . .

The Options for Neutralizing Rogue States

The Libyan case exemplifies the method that compelled a rogue state—with a one-man rule that had been in power for an extended period, used terrorism in the international arena, assisted the terrorist acts of a large number of organizations around the world, and was directly exposed in this participation—to surrender to a coordinated counterpolicy adopted by an international coalition led by countries with high international status. Through effective sanctions leveled under the auspices of the UN [United Nations], the state was impelled to transform its policy with regard to terrorism. Later, this coordinated counterpolicy also resulted in a change in the country's policy on the development of weapons of mass destruction.

It is important to emphasize that the international coalition against Libya emerged against the backdrop of a number of processes unfolding in the international arena, most importantly the formative events that led to the exposure of Libya's direct involvement in the murder of numerous citizens of several nationalities. The disintegration of the Soviet Union and the crystallization of a one-superpower world, and the 1991 formation of an international coalition to resist the aggression of [Iraqi leader] Saddam Hussein, who was seen by the international community as an uncontrolled tyrant leading a rogue state in terms of terrorism and non-conventional weapons, also contributed to the evolution of coordinated international action to restrain Qaddafi's policy of terrorism. . . .

The international community, led by the United States and Europe, faces a major challenge that entails influencing rogue states, first and foremost Iran and Syria, to transform their policies with regard to terrorism and non-conventional weapons. The Libyan model is one option of how to meet this challenge.

> "Terrorists are not cancers on the body
> of a weakened nation-state that die
> when the state dies. Rather, they are
> migrating parasites that temporarily
> occupy hosts."

Terrorists Are Stateless Martyrs

Benjamin R. Barber

In the following viewpoint Benjamin R. Barber maintains that attacks against rogue states believed to support terrorists fail to eradicate terrorism because terrorists are not a part of the nations they occupy. Instead, terrorists are parasites that simply move on to another state after such attacks. The doctrine of preventive war, which justifies U.S. military assaults against nations that support terrorists, neither promotes peace nor prevents terrorism, he claims. Barber is Kekst Professor of Civil Society at the University of Maryland, director of the New York office of the Democracy Collaborative, and the author of many books, including The Truth of Power: Intellectual Affairs in the Clinton White House, *and* Fear's Empire: War, Terrorism and Democracy.

As you read, consider the following questions:

Benjamin R. Barber, "Our War's Mistaken Premise," *Washington Post*, September 14, 2003. Reproduced by permission of the author.

1. According to Barber, when was the doctrine of preventive war announced?

2. In Barber's view, where did the al Qaeda terrorist cadres move after their Taliban host was defeated?

3. What Bush administration strategy against terrorism does Barber believe has had more success than the doctrine of preventive war?

President [George W. Bush] is changing tactics. Forget weapons of mass destruction, the war in Iraq is about terrorism; time to go back to the United Nations [U.N.] to get some help with the military occupation and with paying the $87 billion reckoning for staying in Afghanistan and Iraq that is now being acknowledged. But he has reaffirmed his strategic vision: It is America's strategy of preventive war against rogue states, the very concept that has been the source of America's inability so far to defeat terrorism or establish anything resembling democracy in Afghanistan and Iraq.

That is the powerful lesson that can be drawn from the carnage at U.N. headquarters in Baghdad, from the emerging insurrectionary alliance between Baathists[1] and radical Muslim groups, the reemergence of the Taliban[2] and its politics of assassination in Afghanistan, and the renewed rise of sectarian militia forces in both Iraq and Afghanistan.

The Failure of Preventive War

To fully understand America's failure, we have to back up to 9/11 [the terrorist attacks of September 11, 2001]. Preventive war, the novel national-security doctrine announced after 9/11, exempted the United States from the obligation to justify war on grounds of self-defense or imminent threat. It promulgated a new right "to act against emerging threats before they

1. A pan-Arab socialist political party active principally in Syria and Iraq.
2. A fundamentalist Islamic militia that in 1996 took over Afghanistan and set up an Islamist government. U.S. military forces ousted the Taliban in 2001.

Today's Stateless, Global Terrorists

Today's cross-border [terrorist] groups have no . . . attachment to territory. They view territory expediently, as a base from which they can organise their campaigns and plot their attacks. The new breed of Islamic terror groups are, according to [foreign policy experts Ray] Takeyh and [Nikolas] Gvosdev, 'explicitly global'—in the sense that they have broadly anti-Western views rather than locally defined objectives, and their members hail from different states rather than from a distinct community with distinct interests. For these 'global' terrorists, territory is merely a place from which they can plot.

Brendan O'Neill, Spiked Online,
July 24, 2003.
www.spiked-online.com.

are fully formed," to "act preemptively" against states that harbor or support terrorism. It is this strategic doctrine, and not tactics or policies on the ground in Iraq and Afghanistan, that is now failing so catastrophically.

The war on terrorism remains the Bush administration's ultimate rationale. The administration continues to insist that "in Iraq, we took another essential step in the war on terror" (Vice President [Dick] Cheney), that "military and rehabilitation efforts now under way in Iraq are an essential part of the war on terror" (Deputy Defense Secretary Paul Wolfowitz), that Saddam Hussein's Iraq was a "terror regime" and that the ongoing war there today must be understood as part of the war on terror (President Bush).

Yet terrorism is flourishing—not just in Saudi Arabia, Morocco, Kenya and Indonesia but in Afghanistan, where the Taliban were supposedly defeated, and in Iraq, where, prior to the war, there was no sponsored international terrorism at all.

Understanding Terrorism

The harrowing truth is that preventive attacks on "rogue states" and "those who sponsor or harbor terrorism" fail because they are premised on a fatal misunderstanding of what terrorism is and how it operates. In operational terms, terrorists are not cancers on the body of a weakened nation-state that die when the state dies. Rather, they are migrating parasites that temporarily occupy hosts (rogue states, weak governments, even transparent democracies). When a given host is destroyed or rendered immune to such parasites, they opportunistically move on to another host—ever ready to reoccupy the earlier host if it is revived as a "friendly" regime. With their Taliban host eliminated, al Qaeda [terrorist] cadres moved on—to the Afghan hinterland, to Pakistan, to Morocco, Indonesia, Saudi Arabia, Nigeria, the Philippines, maybe back to Hamburg [Germany] and to those places identified early on as harboring the terrorists of 9/11, Florida and New Jersey, and now back to Baghdad [Iraq] and Kabul [Afghanistan].

Terrorists are not states, they use states. As Defense Secretary Donald Rumsfeld himself said after 9/11, in words he has apparently forgotten, "the people who do this don't lose, don't have high-value targets. They have networks and fanaticism." Because they are "stateless martyrs," as happy to die as to kill, terrorists cannot be defeated through preventive military victories over countries that may share their agendas or harbor their agents. They have neither an address to which complaints and troops can be sent nor conventional "interests" that can be negotiated or penalized. Al Qaeda is in effect a malevolent NGO [nongovernmental organization].

Terrorists are, in the president's words, "enemies of the civilized world." But what makes the world civilized is its adherence to the rule of law, its insistence that it will not attack adversaries, however evil, unless first attacked by them, its reliance on multilateral cooperation and international courts rather than unilateral military force and the right of the strongest.

The president's policies meet fear with fear, trying to "shock and awe"[1] adversaries into submission. But fear is terrorism's medium, not ours. Democracies that respect the rule of law cannot win wars unilaterally and in defiance of international law—not when the enemy has no policy but chaos, no end but annihilation (including its own).

[Former president] Harry Truman once said that all war prevents is peace. Preventive war has neither created peace nor preempted terrorism. The intelligence and police cooperation that the Bush administration has quietly been engaged in has, to the contrary, had more success. But it is directed at terrorists, not rogue states, and it has succeeded through the very cooperation and multilateralism that unilateral preventive war undermines.

Pursuing preventive war at a growing cost in American lives and money against regimes the Bush administration doesn't like, or countries that brutalize their own people, may appeal to American virtue, but it undermines American security.

The only proper way the United States can honor both its national interests and those who have died in this war and its aftermath is to abandon its failed preventive war doctrine and rejoin the world it has tried in vain to pacify through unilateral preemptive force.

---

1. A military strategy whereby a government employs spectacular displays of power in order to intimidate an adversary.

"There is a cluster of nation-states . . . that pose continuing threats to their own inhabitants and to stability and peace in the world."

Rogue Nations Threaten International Peace

World Peace Foundation

According to the World Peace Foundation in the following viewpoint, true rogue states are both repressive and aggressive. Repressive states, the foundation maintains, deny their own people human rights and political freedom. Aggressive states possess or seek to possess weapons of mass destruction, sponsor terrorism, and threaten or attack their neighbors, the author claims. Those states that pose the most serious threat to international peace include North Korea, Iran, Saudi Arabia, Syria, Uzbekistan, and Zimbabwe, the foundation asserts. The World Peace Foundation studies and participates in state conflict resolution.

As you read, consider the following questions:

1. In addition to possessing WMD, sponsoring terrorists, and attacking neighboring states, what does the World Peace Foundation claim constitutes aggression?

World Peace Foundation, "Identifying Rogue States: Issues of Policy and Action," *Policy Brief #3*, November 9, 2004. Reproduced by permission.

2. According to the authors, whom do super- or regularly aggressive nations terrorize in addition to their neighbors?

3. What states threaten their own nationals but do not yet undermine world order, as stated by the foundation?

Which are the true "rogue" states? What is "rogueness" in the international arena? Do rogue states share certain common characteristics? If so, what should be done to curtail rogue states? How can rogue states be encouraged to behave less roguishly?

Repression and Aggression

A far-ranging World Peace Foundation project on rogue states concluded that nation-states qualify as rogue states when and if they rank very high on two scales: repression and aggression. Those nation-states that systematically oppress their own people, deny human rights and civil liberties, severely truncate political freedom, and prevent meaningful individual economic opportunity, are easy to stigmatize. When they also starve their own people, the designation of a nation-state as a serial repressor comes readily.

Along the axis of aggression, many (but not all) of the most repressive nation-states in the world also rate high. If a nation-state possesses weapons of mass destruction [WMD], or seeks to attain WMD, they threaten world order and are by definition aggressive. Sponsors of terrorism are obviously aggressive. Lower down on the same scale are nation-states that attack or threaten their neighbors militarily. Then there are those nation-states that traffic in narcotics, launder illicit funds, ship small arms illegally, interfere with the free trade of their neighbors, or otherwise behave boorishly in their sub-regions. Those nation-states, even without the taint of terror or WMD, may destabilize or poison their regional political or economic environments.

Acting Outside International Law

The moniker "rogue state" . . . does seem to be useful for understanding the behavior of certain regimes in light of international law. In a sense, a rogue state is one that does not follow the rules. While almost all states may at times violate international legal rules, a rogue state would be a perennial violator. It would, in essence, be a state whose identity is to some extent defined by acting outside of the standard rules of international law.

Anthony Clark Arend, New England Law Review, *Summer 2002.*

A very few repressive states are only dangerous to themselves. That is, their ruling classes prey only on their citizens, and only occasionally reach out across national borders. But no super-aggressive, or even regularly aggressive, nation-state does not attack its own people in a seriously kleptocratic or oppressive manner.

There is a cluster of nation-states, in other words, that pose continuing threats to their own inhabitants and to stability and peace in the world. Those are the rogue states. Or, to use language that is less emotive, those are the nation-states suffering from acute repressive-aggressive disorder. Nation-states with that malady pose unacceptable risks to world order—to peace in our time.

Identifying Rogue States

The World Peace Foundation rogue states project is refining its criteria for repression and aggression. For now, the most repressive states in the world, listed alphabetically, are deemed to be: Belarus, Burma, Equatorial Guinea, Iran, North Korea, Saudi Arabia, Syria, Togo, Turkmenistan, Tunisia, Uzbekistan, and Zimbabwe. The project intends to rank-order those nation-states (and others to be added, with some possibly subtracted) according to quantitative assessments being constructed.

Likewise, among those dangerous states, North Korea and Iran rank at the highest pole of aggression. Syria follows. Then there is a grouping of less threatening but still aggressive states such as Saudi Arabia, Uzbekistan, and Zimbabwe. Belarus, Burma, Equatorial Guinea, Togo, Tunisia, and Turkmenistan threaten their own nationals much more than they currently undermine world order. Even if one or more of this last group may harbor a terrorist cell, or engage in drug trafficking or money laundering, the scale of such operations so far is limited and not beyond "yellow" in terms of any world order alert. The first three aggressive states above, however, are much more hostile, as are the three who follow, especially in their own neighborhoods.

There are a few other nation-states that are or have been aggressive, but may not necessarily oppress their own people harshly. Further investigation may add new names to the lists above. Moreover, the project knows that other nation-states are repressive, possibly in some cases even more repressive than some of the nation-states singled out for obloquy in this Policy Brief. The Foundation project intends to develop tougher and more thorough quantitative criteria to distinguish degrees of repression and degrees of aggression in today's world.

Given a responsibility to protect the weak and the preyed upon in countries like those listed here, Washington and the United Nations both need to craft new policies to intervene diplomatically or otherwise before the next Rwandas and Darfurs occur.[1] Bright lines of behavior need to be established

1. In Rwanda an estimated 937,000 Tutsis and moderate Hutus were killed largely by two extremist Hutu militia groups during a period of a hundred days in 1994. In the Darfur region of western Sudan, a conflict between local non-Arab tribes and the Janjaweed, a government-supported militia, has led to the starvation or murder of an unknown number (estimates vary from 180,000 to 300,000) of local tribespeople. Millions have been displaced from both nations.

across which repressive states step at their peril. Being a repressive state is in its own way a decisive threat to a peaceful world in addition to being an intolerable burden on a country's own inhabitants.

There are established policies regarding the most aggressive WMD and terror threats. Less so are there well-crafted policies to curb exporters of enmity, crime, drugs, weapons, and so on. But if there are nation-states that deserve to be called rogues, so there must be policies that Washington, Brussels, and Moscow can devise to reduce the destabilizing threats posed by the real rogue states of the world. The World Peace Foundation will develop appropriate policy options in collaboration with a range of academic, diplomatic, intelligence, and military experts.

*"The United States government has be-
come the sole 'rogue elephant' of international law and politics."*

The United States Threatens
International Peace

Francis A. Boyle

*Under the leadership of George W. Bush, the United States has
become a rogue state that threatens international peace, argues
Francis A. Boyle in the following viewpoint. According to Boyle,
the United States routinely withdraws from or refuses to become
a signatory to arms control and other international treaties.
What is more, he claims, America has plans to use nuclear weapons against other nations. Boyle is an international law and human rights professor at the University of Illinois College of Law.*

As you read, consider the following questions:

1. According to Boyle, what event did the Bush administration exploit when it announced its plans to abandon the
   ABM treaty?
2. What Pentagon behavior does the author think is an
   ominous sign of the times?

Francis A. Boyle, "The Rogue Elephant," *Synthesis/Regeneration*, Spring 2003. Reproduced by permission.

3. According to the Nuclear Posture Review, in wars between what nations must the Pentagon draw up nuclear
war–fighting plans?

When George Bush, Jr. came to power in January of 2001,
he proceeded to implement foreign affairs and defense
policies that were every bit as radical, extreme and excessive as
those of the Reagan/Bush administrations had, starting in
January of 1981. Upon his installation, Bush Jr.'s "compassionate conservatism" quickly revealed itself to be nothing more
than reactionary Machiavellianism—as if there had been any
real doubt about this during the presidential election campaign. Even the Bush, Jr. cast of Machiavellian characters was
pretty much the same as the original Reagan/Bush foreign affairs and defense "experts." It was *déjà vu* all over again, as
[baseball legend] Yogi Berra aptly put it.

International Legal Nihilism

In quick succession the world saw these Bush, Jr. Leaguers re-
pudiate:

- the Kyoto Protocol on global warming,

- the International Criminal Court,

- the Comprehensive Test Ban Treaty (CTBT),

- an international convention to regulate the trade in
small arms,

- a verification Protocol for the Biological Weapons Convention,

- an international convention to regulate and reduce
smoking,

- the World Conference Against Racism, and

- the Anti-Ballistic Missile Systems Treaty [ABM].

To date, the Bush administration has not found an international convention that it did like. The only exception was the shameless exploitation of the September 11, 2001 tragedy in order to get the US House of Representatives to give Bush Jr. so-called "fast-track" trade negotiation authority.

More ominously, once into office the Bush administration adopted an incredibly belligerent posture towards the People's Republic of China (PRC), publicly identifying the PRC as America's foremost competitor/opponent into the 21st century.

Then their needlessly pugnacious approach towards the downing of a US spy plane in China with the death of a Chinese pilot only exacerbated already tense US/Chinese relations. Next, the Bush administration decided to sell high-tech weapons to Taiwan in violation of the USA/PRC Joint Communiqué of August 17, 1982 that had been negotiated and concluded earlier by the Reagan/Bush administration.

Finally came Bush Jr.'s breathtaking statement that the United States would defend Taiwan in the event of an attack by the PRC irrespective of Article I, Section 8, Clause 11 of the United States Constitution, expressly reserving to Congress alone the right to declare war. President Jimmy Carter had long-ago terminated the US-Taiwan self-defense treaty.

The Withdrawal from the ABM Treaty

Then, as had been foreshadowed, whispered, and hinted at, came the announcement on December 13, 2001 by the Bush Jr. administration of their intent to withdraw the US from the ABM Treaty, effective within six months. Of course, it was sheer coincidence that the Pentagon released their self-styled Osama bin Laden [terrorist] video just as Bush Jr. himself publicly announced his indefensible decision to withdraw from the ABM Treaty. This withdrawal would allow Bush Jr. to pursue his National Missile Defense (NMD) Program; the successor to the Reagan/Bush Star Wars dream.

This Isn't the Real America

Instead of [the American] tradition of espousing peace as a national priority unless our security is directly threatened, we have proclaimed a policy of "preemptive war," an unabridged right to attack other nations unilaterally to change an unsavory regime or for other purposes. When there are serious differences with other nations, we brand them as international pariahs and refuse to permit direct discussions to resolve disputes. Regardless of the costs, there are determined efforts by top US leaders to exert American imperial dominance throughout the world.

Jimmy Carter, Los Angeles Times, *November 14, 2005.*

Predictably, the bin Laden video back-staged this major pro-nuclear announcement. Once again the terrible national tragedy of September 11 was shamelessly exploited in order to justify a reckless decision that had already been made for other reasons long before.

Then, on January 25, 2002, the Pentagon promptly conducted a sea-based NMD test in gross violation of Article 5(I) of the ABM Treaty without waiting for the required six months to expire. In doing so, the administration drove a proverbial nail into the coffin of the ABM Treaty before its body was even legally dead.

The US withdrawal from the ABM Treaty threatens the very existence of other seminal arms control treaties and regimes such as the Nuclear Non-Proliferation Treaty (NPT) and the Biological Weapons Convention. These treaties have similar withdrawal clauses. The prospect of yet another multilateral and destabilizing nuclear arms race now stares humanity directly in the face. The Bush Jr. administration is preparing for the quick resumption of nuclear testing at the Nevada test site in outright defiance of the CTBT regime and NPT Article VI. The entire edifice of international agreements regulating, reducing, and eliminating weapons of mass extermination (WME) has been shaken to its very core. Now the Pentagon and the CIA [Central Intelligence Agency] are back into the dirty business of researching, developing and testing biological weapons and biological agents that are clearly prohibited by the Biological Weapons Convention and its US domestic implementing legislation, the Biological Weapons Anti-Terrorism Act of 1989.

The US First-Strike Nuclear Strategy

With the collapse of the Soviet Union and the impoverishment of Russia leaving the United States as the world's "only superpower" or "hyperpower," we are getting to the point where only the United States has the capability to launch an offensive first-strike strategic nuclear weapons attack. For that reason, deploying the so-called "National Missile Defense" (NMD) has become a critical objective of the United States government. NMD is not really needed to shoot down a stray missile from some so-called "rogue state." Rather, US NMD is essential for mopping up any residual Russian or Chinese strategic nuclear weapons that might survive a US first-strike with strategic nuclear weapons systems.

The successful deployment of NMD will finally provide the United States with what it has always sought: the capacity to launch a successful offensive first-strike strategic nuclear attack, coupled with the capability to neutralize a Russian and/or Chinese retaliatory nuclear attack. At that point, the United States will proceed to use this capability to enforce its hegemonial will upon the rest of the world.

Strategic nuclear "thinkers," such as Harvard's Thomas Schelling, call this doctrine "compellance" as opposed to "deterrence." With NMD the world will become dominated by this US "compellance" strategy.

Honest Nuclear War-Mongering

Consequently, it should come as no surprise that the historically covert intent of America's nuclear "deterrence policy" should now come to light through almost off-the-cuff remarks such as those by the omnipresent US Deputy Secretary of Defense Paul Wolfowitz appearing in the January 9, 2002 edition of the *New York Times.*

Wolfowitz admitted that the current US practice of so-called nuclear "deterrence" is in fact really based upon "an almost exclusive emphasis on offensive nuclear forces." To reiterate, since this deserves emphasis: The US Deputy Secretary of Defense has publicly admitted and conceded that "almost" all US nuclear forces are really "offensive" and not really "defenses." Of course, the peace movement and informed American public knew this was true all along. Nonetheless, it should be regarded as an ominous sign of the times that the Pentagon has become so brazen that it is publicly admitting US nuclear criminality to the entire world. The arrogance of the Hyperpower!

A Nuremberg Crime Against Peace

Then, writing in the March 10, 2002 edition of the *Los Angeles Times,* defense analyst William Arkin revealed the leaked contents of the Bush Jr. administration's Nuclear Posture Review (NPR) that it had just transmitted to Congress on January 8, 2002. The Bush Jr. administration has ordered the Pentagon to draw up war plans for the first-use of nuclear weapons against seven states: the so-called "axis of evil." This "axis" includes Iran, Iraq, and North Korea, Libya as well as Syria, Russia, and China, which are armed with nuclear weapons.

This component of the Bush, Jr. NPR incorporates the Clinton administration's 1997 nuclear war-fighting plans against so-called "rogue states" set forth in Presidential Decision Directive 60. These warmed-over nuclear war plans targeting these five non-nuclear states expressly violate the so-called "negative security assurances" given by the United States as an express condition for the renewal and indefinite extension of the Nuclear Non-Proliferation Treaty (NPT) by all of its non-nuclear weapons states parties in 1995. . . .

Article 6 of the 1945 Nuremberg Charter and the Principles of International Law recognized in the Charter of the Nuremberg Tribunal and in the Judgment of the Tribunal both . . . clearly provide that the "planning" or "preparation" of a war in violation of international "assurances" such as the aforementioned US negative security assurance constitutes a Nuremberg Crime against Peace. Such is the Bush Jr. NPR!

The Rogue Elephant of International Law and Politics

Equally reprehensible from a legal perspective was the NPR's call for the Pentagon to draft nuclear war-fighting plans for first nuclear strikes: (1) against alleged nuclear/chemical/ biological "materials" or "facilities," (2) "against targets able to withstand non-nuclear attack," and (3) "in the event of surprising military developments," whatever that means. According to the NPR, the Pentagon must also draw up nuclear war-fighting plans to intervene with nuclear weapons in wars between (1) China and Taiwan, (2) Israel and the Arab states, (3) North Korea and South Korea, and (4) Israel and Iraq. It is obvious as to whose side the United States will actually plan to intervene with the first-use nuclear weapons. Today, the Bush Jr. administration accelerates its plans for launching an apocalyptic military aggression against Iraq, deliberately raising the specter of a US first-strike nuclear attack upon that long-suffering country and its people.

The Bush Jr. administration is making it crystal clear to all its chosen adversaries around the world that it is fully prepared to cross the threshold of actually using nuclear weapons that has prevailed since the US criminal bombings of Hiroshima and Nagasaki in 1945. Yet more proof of the fact that the US has officially abandoned "deterrence" for "compel-lance" in order to rule the future world of the third millennium.

The Bush, Jr. administration has obviously become a "threat to the peace" within the meaning of UN Charter article 39. It must be countermanded by the UN Security Council acting under Chapter VII of the UN Charter. In the event of a US veto of such "enforcement action" by the Security Council, then the UN General Assembly must deal with the Bush Jr. administration by invoking its Uniting for Peace Resolution of 1950.

There very well could be some itty-bitty "rogue states" lurking out there somewhere in the Third World, but today the United States government has become the sole "rogue elephant" of international law and politics. For the good of all humanity, America must be restrained.

Periodical Bibliography

The following articles have been selected to supplement the diverse views presented in this chapter.

Anthony Clark Arend
"International Law and Rogue States: The Failure of the Charter Framework," *New England Law Review*, Summer 2002.

Jimmy Carter
"This Isn't the Real America," *Los Angeles Times*, November 14, 2005.

Sam T. Cohen and Joseph D. Douglass Jr.
"The Rogue Nuclear Threat," *American Spectator*, March/April 2003.

Economist
"A World Wide Web of Nuclear Danger," February 28, 2004.

Madhavee Inamdar
"Rogue Nations and WMD: Hiroshima and Nagasaki Remembered," *Foreign Policy in Focus*, December 12, 2002.

Lee Kass
"The Growing Syrian Missile Threat," *Middle East Quarterly*, Fall 2005.

Paul Mervis
"Let Them Have Nukes," *Spectator*, November 5, 2005.

New Scientist
"The Final Straw for a Fragile Treaty?" June 19, 2004.

Brendan O'Neill
"Cross-Border Terrorism: A Mess Made by the West," *Spiked Online*, July 24, 2003. www.spiked-online.com.

David E. Sanger
"Going Nuclear?" *New York Times Upfront*, January 24, 2005.

Henry Sokolski
"Taking Proliferation Seriously," *Policy Review*, October/November 2003.

CHAPTER 3

How Do Rogue Nations Threaten Human Rights?

Chapter Preface

One of the controversies concerning rogue nations is how best to address human rights violations in nations that also pose a nuclear threat. The debate over the appropriate U.S. strategy toward North Korea is illustrative. North Korea is considered one of the most egregious human rights violators, and it is also thought to have developed nuclear weapons. While some analysts argue that regime change is necessary to promote human rights and put an end to North Korea's nuclear threat, others contend that such as policy would further threaten the human rights of the North Korean people.

After the death of Communist North Korean leader Kim Il Sung and a devastating North Korean famine, many believed that North Korea would open its economy, improve its human rights record, and abandon its quest to conquer South Korea. However, Kim Jong Il, the son of Kim Il Sung, realized that such reform would mean the end of his empire. Diplomatic efforts by the Bill Clinton and George W. Bush administrations failed to put an end to his repressive regime, and Kim Jong Il has consistently broken his promises to improve human rights and end North Korea's nuclear weapons program.

Some commentators argue that replacing the regime of Kim Jong Il would be the best strategy to protect human rights and end the nation's nuclear threat. Foreign policy analyst Nicholas Eberstadt maintains, "American policy should be actively engaged in planning for a successful transition to a post–Kim Jong Il Korea." Efforts to trade aid for reform, these analysts claim, will continue to meet with failure. Author Jasper Becker asserts, "There are those . . . who think that such a deal would be the best way to reduce tensions and to wean Pyongyang [North Korea's capital] off the habits of a rogue state. But the analysis is flawed." Eberstadt agrees, "We are exceedingly unlikely to talk—or to bribe—the current North

Korean government out of its nuclear quest. Talk and bribery have been tried for nearly 15 years—with miserable results."

Others contend that regime change will only exacerbate the human rights problem in North Korea. According to professor Kenneth Liebenthal, "A coup by the military or police in North Korea could topple Mr. Kim only to replace him with another dictator. . . . The human rights situation in the North would not improve and there is no reason to believe that these individuals would prove more sensible than Mr. Kim has been." Foreign policy analyst John Feffer maintains that "the Bush administration's approach to North Korea[n] human rights may well put the intended beneficiaries at greater risk in order to achieve a larger and putatively nobler cause." Feffer continues, "Inconsistent and hypocritical, the United States has become evangelical in its policy on North Korean human rights. . . . They will flirt with apocalypse to get the rapture of regime change, and North Koreans—who have suffered so much already—will bear the brunt of it."

The debate over whether regime change will promote North Korean human rights continues. The authors in this chapter explore human rights abuses in North Korea and other rogue nations.

> *"North Korea has such a long record of systematic [human rights] abuses that it is one of the most repressive governments in the world."*

North Korea Represses Freedom

Kay Seok

The North Korean government is brutal and repressive, claims Kay Seok in the following viewpoint. According to Seok, the government not only suppresses freedom of the press and religion but also imprisons those who oppose the government. Many North Koreans die in prison due to cruel and inhuman treatment, she asserts. Those who escape to China, Seok argues, are hunted and brought back to North Korea, where they are tortured and often executed. Seok, director of communications for Human Rights Watch in New York, tracks abuses in North Korea.

As you read, consider the following questions:

1. According to Seok, how did the North Korean government respond when confronted with its human rights record?

Kay Seok, "Put Human Rights First in North Korea," *Observer*, September 11, 2004. Reproduced by permission of the author.

2. In the author's opinion, what commonly happens to the families of those accused of political crimes?

3. In addition to addressing issues of international security, what does Seok believe is necessary to improve relations with North Korea?

North Korea stands at a crossroads. After half a century of rigid isolation and its notoriously failed policy of "self-reliance," this impoverished country has cautiously begun to seek better diplomatic ties and more foreign investment. . . .

When confronted on its human rights record, the regime of the "Dear Leader" Kim Jong Il, who has proved a shrewdly capable dictator, has always flatly denied that a problem exists. After Human Rights Watch and others submitted reports on North Korea to the United Nations human rights commission [in 2003], the government of the Democratic People's Republic of Korea (DPRK)—as North Korea is officially known—responded with a terse English-language statement: "There exists no 'human rights issue' in DPRK as all its people form a big family and live in harmony helping and leading one another forward under the man-centred socialist system."

A Record of Abuses

In reality, North Korea has such a long record of systematic abuses that it is one of the most repressive governments in the world. There is no freedom of the press or religion. There is no labour activism, no independent civil society and no political opposition permitted. Basic services, such as access to health care and education, are parcelled out according to a classification scheme that divides people into three groups—"core," "wavering," and "hostile"—based on the government's assessment of their and their family's political loyalty.

But the worst abuses occur when an individual is suspected of having tried to exercise one of the many basic freedoms that are prohibited. Perceived troublemakers are ar-

The North Korean Gulag

In the past three decades, some 400,000 North Koreans are believed to have perished in the gulag [prison system]. Yet relatively little is known about the [prison] camps, which are sealed off from international scrutiny. *U.S. News* tracked down five former prisoners and guards who managed to defect to South Korea, and they describe a world of routine horror: beatings, crippling torture, hunger, slave-style labor, executions.

Thomas Omestad, U.S. News & World Report, June 23, 2003.

rested, permitted no contact with family or legal counsel, forced to confess under often brutal torture, and sent to prison. Those in prison face cruel, inhuman, and degrading treatment; many die because of mistreatment, malnutrition and lack of medical care.

For political crimes, whether actual or perceived, it is common for the perpetrator's entire family to be sent to forced labour camps, sometimes for the rest of their lives. Even if the families avoid such a fate, they are often barred from good jobs or higher education. The number of political prisoners held in prisons is reckoned to be as many as 200,000—nearly 1 per cent of the entire population.

Hunting Expatriates

Abuses of North Koreans are not necessarily restricted by the country's borders. The famine in the mid-1990s, which may have killed as many as two million people, drove tens of thousands of North Koreans across the border into China to find food.

Many live in hiding today as North Korean agents hunt and repatriate them for the crime of leaving their country without state permission. Instead of treating them as refugees under international law, Chinese authorities arrest them as illegal immigrants. Women and children often become victims of violence, trafficking and sexual slavery, but have no legal means of redress.

Once repatriated, North Koreans face detention, torture and even execution if they are found to have had contact with Westerners or South Koreans, especially missionaries. Such executions are reportedly carried out in public, often in the presence of children. Meanwhile, North Korea's children have been by far the biggest victims of the famine. Many lost their parents to hunger, have become stunted for life themselves, and are reportedly spending more time trying to find food than in classrooms.

But Pyongyang [North Korea's capital] seems to realize that things cannot go on as they were. It has opened diplomatic relations with 19 countries in the past few years, including Britain and a host of other European nations. [In 2003] it launched a market-oriented economic reform. There are now bustling new markets in Pyongyang and huge billboards advertising consumer goods. A South Korean conglomerate is building a new multimillion [dollar] industrial complex in southwestern North Korea, which the government hopes will bring in more foreign currency. . . .

It is essential to remember that moves towards building better diplomatic relations and more foreign investment can be meaningful only if, in addition to addressing issues of international security, they also result in concrete improvements for the North Korean people. Britain can make a difference if it gains commitments from Pyongyang to allow humanitarian organizations better access within the country to deliver badly needed food and health care; if it can gain access for the United Nations and non-governmental organizations to North Korean prisons—and, above all, if North Korea agrees to take seriously the rights of its people to fundamental freedoms.

> *"Despite the porous borders, the Iranian Mullahs continue to oppress their people, and women and children undoubtedly suffer the most."*

Iran Violates Women's Rights

Sam Brownback

In the following viewpoint, excerpted from a speech delivered on the U.S. Senate floor in June 2005, Sam Brownback, U.S. senator from Kansas, argues that the repressive Iranian regime violates the rights of women. The Iranian government has declared women to be inferior, Brownback maintains. Young girls, he asserts, can be forced to marry before they reach puberty, and women have no right to divorce or retain custody of their children if their husbands die or divorce them, he contends.

As you read, consider the following questions:

1. In Brownback's opinion, in what way is Iran a porous society?
2. According to the author, how did some Iranian women rebel against the Mullahs' strict laws?
3. How might major change be promoted in Iran, in the author's view?

Sam Brownback, "Speech on the Floor of the United States Senate," June 16, 2005.

I rise today to speak on an issue that is of great importance to me and an issue that should be discussed more broadly by the United States and our European partners. I come to speak about the crisis in Iran—but the crisis I want to discuss today is not the nuclear crisis. The crisis is that of the human rights situation that faces millions of Iranians every day. While almost every Iranian feels the oppression of the regime, today I will focus on Iranian women who are victims at the hands of the regime by virtue of their gender.

A Dismal Human Rights Record

I am mindful of the hardship faced by individuals living under authoritarian regimes or dictatorships. Across the board, Iran's human rights record is dismal. The Iranian regime employs all of the levers of power to crush dissent, resorting in every form of persecution—even so far as execution. No effort is spared to silence opposition.

In some ways Iran is a porous society, with information flowing in and out via the Internet, telephone, and even satellite broadcasting. My office has received e-mails and pictures from individuals in Iran, a far different mechanism for communication than can be found in other tyrannical regimes around the world. Despite the porous society, the regime continues to clamp down on independent media.

In the absence of any meaningful accountability, the government of Iran's dismal rights record has actually worsened, according to the State Department's latest Country Reports on Human Rights Practices. Severe restrictions are placed on freedom of speech, press, assembly, association, and religion. With respect to religion, the U.S. Commission on International Religious Freedom has concluded that, "the government of Iran engages in or tolerates systematic, ongoing, and egregious violations of religious freedom, including prolonged detention and executions based primarily or entirely upon the religion of the accused." Accordingly, the State Department

The Politics of Misogyny

Misogyny is a primary characteristic of the fundamentalist ideology ruling Iran. These tyrants rely on physiological traits to measure, separate and categorize people. Utilizing Hitlerian logic, women are physically and intellectually weaker than men. The establishment and maintenance of supremacy of the sort defined by the fundamentalist regime requires an inferior class. In the mullahs' view, Iranian women, despite their articulate and vocal objections, should be forced into this role.

Roya Johnson, American Thinker, *April 5, 2005.*

has designated Iran as a "Country of Particular Concern" each year since 1999 under the International Religious Freedom Act.

Gender Apartheid

[Former *NBC Nightly News* anchor] Tom Brokaw recently traveled to Iran and reported on women attempting to rebel against the Mullahs' strict laws by wearing colorful head scarves. One of the women he interviewed, however, suggested that pink lipstick and a matching head scarf were pushing the outer limits for Iranian women. It is evident that, despite the porous borders, the Iranian Mullahs continue to oppress their people, and women and children undoubtedly suffer the most.

Here are a few examples of the gender apartheid that currently exists in Iran that I received from the Alliance for Iranian Women:

- The State Department has reported that, "The testimony of a woman is worth half that of a man in court. The blood money paid to the family of a female crime victim is half the sum paid for a man. A married woman must obtain written consent of her husband before traveling outside the country."

- In his book, Ayatollah [Ruholla] Khomeini requires young girls to be married before they reach puberty.

- A woman does not have the right to divorce her husband, but a man can divorce his wife any time he wishes and without her knowledge.

- Men are allowed to marry four wives and have as many temporary wives as they want and may end the contract at any time. Temporary marriage is often viewed as the Islamic Republic's way of sanctioning male promiscuity outside of marriage.

- Mothers do not get custody of their children when husbands divorce them.

- A widow does not get the custody of her children after the death of her husband. The children will be given to the paternal grandparents or relatives, and the mother has no right to visitation. If the husband has no family, the Mullah of the community takes the custody of the child.

- Daughters get half the inheritance than that of sons.

Iran is rated as a Tier 2 country in this year's "Trafficking in Persons Report." The report states, "Boys from Bangladesh, Pakistan, and Afghanistan are trafficked through Iran to Gulf states, where they are ultimately forced to work as camel jockeys, beggars, or laborers. Afghan women and girls are trafficked to Iran for sexual exploitation, and for sexual and labor exploitation in the context of forced marriage." It was also reported earlier [in 2005] that an 18-year-old handicapped girl, with the mental capacity of an 8-year-old, received a death sentence after her parents forced her into prostitution.

The Importance of Promoting Human Rights

Unfortunately, these stories are far too common. The international community has focused significant amounts of attention on the growing nuclear and terrorism threat that Iran poses to countries like Israel and the U.S. While this is an important focus of U.S. foreign policy, I remain concerned that it could be a short-sighted approach if not coupled with democracy and human rights promotion. If we are to focus simply on [nuclear] proliferation issues and not human rights and democracy, the procurement of such weapons will be left in the hands of tyrants. It is my belief that we should simultaneously build civil society, promote human rights and back the young generation of Iranians who are disillusioned and want change through a referendum.

The country's security and intelligence services are pervasive. As a result, a small circle of clerics—headed by the Supreme Leader—maintains a virtual monopoly of power in Iran. In the face of this abusive regime, courageous individuals and groups do seek change, often at great personal risk.

I have come to the Senate floor just days before the Iranian presidential elections. These elections hold no hope of change for the people. They are elections that will be boycotted in protest, and they are elections that have been manipulated by the Supreme Leader and Council of Guardians.[1] [In June 2005] women in Iran staged a sit-in to protest the disqualification of women from running in the elections. The people of Iran want change. That change will not come through elections, but it will come through strong international support for the very people that protest and boycott the elections.

1. In fact, 60 percent of voters turned out for the run-off election on June 24, 2005, in which Mahmoud Ahmadinejad, a religious conservative with Islamist and populist views, was elected. The election remains controversial.

Iran has a young and vibrant base that, with the support of the international community, could promote major change in Iran and in the region. I would encourage the Iranian-American community to unite and build a strong coalition to further the promotion of democracy and fundamental respect for human rights in Iran. I would encourage members of this body to continuously speak up on behalf of the oppressed in Iran and voice strong support for the people who so desperately want to see democracy flourish.

"The government of Sudan is responsible for 'ethnic cleansing' and crimes against humanity in Darfur."

The Sudanese Government Engages in Genocide

Human Rights Watch

In the following viewpoint Human Rights Watch, an international nongovernmental organization that monitors human rights worldwide, contends that the Sudanese government has led a genocidal campaign against Sudan's Fur, Masalit, and Zaghawa tribes in Darfur. These vicious attacks are a response to rebel groups who are demanding an end to economic oppression and a place in the Arab-ruled Sudanese government, the authors argue. The government and its allies have killed innocent civilians, raped women, enslaved children, and destroyed villages, the authors claim.

As you read, consider the following questions:

1. How has the Sudanese government engaged in ethnic manipulation, according to Human Rights Watch?

Human Rights Watch, "Darfur Destroyed: Ethnic Cleansing by Government and Militia Forces in Western Sudan," *Human Rights Watch*, vol. 16, May 2004. © 2004 Human Rights Watch. Reproduced by permission. Available at: http://hrw.org/reports/2004/sudan0504/

2. In the authors' view, who arrives first and leaves last after attacks in Darfur?

3. How has the Sudanese government responded to allegations of gross human rights abuses, in the authors' opinion?

The government of Sudan is responsible for "ethnic cleansing" and crimes against humanity in Darfur, one of the world's poorest and most inaccessible regions, on Sudan's western border with Chad. The Sudanese government and the Arab "Janjaweed" militias it arms and supports have committed numerous attacks on the civilian populations of the African Fur, Masalit, and Zaghawa ethnic groups. Government forces oversaw and directly participated in massacres, summary executions of civilians—including women and children—burnings of towns and villages, and the forcible depopulation of wide swathes of land long inhabited by the Fur, Masalit, and Zaghawa. The Janjaweed militias, Muslim like the African groups they attack, have destroyed mosques, killed Muslim religious leaders, and desecrated Qorans belonging to their enemies.

The government and its Janjaweed allies have killed thousands of Fur, Masalit, and Zaghawa—often in cold blood—raped women, and destroyed villages, food stocks, and other supplies essential to the civilian population. They have driven more than one million civilians, mostly farmers, into camps and settlements in Darfur, where they live on the very edge of survival, hostage to Janjaweed abuses. More than 110,000 others have fled to neighbouring Chad but the vast majority of war victims remain trapped in Darfur.

Retaliation with Impunity

This conflict has historical roots but escalated in February 2003, when two rebel groups, the Sudan Liberation Army/Movement (SLA/M) and the Justice and Equality Movement

Destroying African Tribal Peoples

The government of Sudan, dominated by the National Islamic Front, is relentlessly, deliberately destroying the African tribal peoples of the region. Indeed, all evidence suggests that what [United Nations] and Western diplomats are diffidently calling "ethnic cleansing" in Darfur, an area the size of France, is actually genocide.

Eric Reeves, In These Times, May 6, 2004.

(JEM) drawn from members of the Fur, Masalit, and Zaghawa ethnic groups, demanded an end to chronic economic marginalization and sought power-sharing within the Arab-ruled Sudanese state. They also sought government action to end the abuses of their rivals, Arab pastoralists who were driven onto African farmlands by drought and desertification—and who had a nomadic tradition of armed militias.

The government has responded to this armed and political threat by targeting the civilian populations from which the rebels were drawn. It brazenly engaged in ethnic manipulation by organizing a military and political partnership with some Arab nomads comprising the Janjaweed; armed, trained, and organized them; and provided effective impunity for all crimes committed.

The government-Janjaweed partnership is characterized by joint attacks on civilians rather than on the rebel forces. These attacks are carried out by members of the Sudanese military and by Janjaweed wearing uniforms that are virtually indistinguishable from those of the army.

Although Janjaweed always outnumber regular soldiers, during attacks the government forces usually arrive first and leave last. In the words of one displaced villager, "They [the soldiers] see everything" that the Janjaweed are doing. "They come with them, they fight with them and they leave with them."

Destruction and Depopulation

The government-Janjaweed attacks are frequently supported by the Sudanese air force. Many assaults have decimated small farming communities, with death tolls sometimes approaching one hundred people. Most are unrecorded.

Human Rights Watch spent twenty-five days in and on the edges of West Darfur, documenting abuses in rural areas that were previously well-populated with Masalit and Fur farmers. Since August 2003, wide swathes of their homelands, among the most fertile in the region, have been burned and depopulated. With rare exceptions, the countryside is now emptied of its original Masalit and Fur inhabitants. Everything that can sustain and succour life—livestock, food stores, wells and pumps, blankets and clothing—has been looted or destroyed. Villages have been torched not randomly, but systematically—often not once, but twice.

The uncontrolled presence of Janjaweed in the burned countryside, and in burned and abandoned villages, has driven civilians into camps and settlements outside the larger towns, where the Janjaweed kill, rape, and pillage—even stealing emergency relief items—with impunity.

Denial and Deception

Despite international calls for investigations into allegations of gross human rights abuses, the government has responded by denying any abuses while attempting to manipulate and stem information leaks. It has limited reports from Darfur in the national press, restricted international media access, and has tried to obstruct the flow of refugees into Chad. Only after significant delays and international pressure, were two high-level UN [United Nations] assessment teams permitted to enter Darfur. The government has promised unhindered humanitarian access, but has failed to deliver. Instead, recent reports of government tampering with mass graves and other evidence suggest the government is fully aware of the immensity of its crimes and is now attempting to cover up any record.

With the rainy season starting in late May and the ensuing logistical difficulties exacerbated by Darfur's poor roads and infrastructure, any international monitoring of the shaky April [2004] ceasefire and continuing human rights abuses, as well as access to humanitarian assistance, will become more difficult. The United States Agency for International Development has warned that unless the Sudanese government breaks with past practice and grants full and immediate humanitarian access, at least 100,000 war-affected civilians could die in Darfur from lack of food and from disease.[1]

The international community, which so far has been slow to exert all possible pressure on the Sudanese government to reverse the ethnic cleansing and end the associated crimes against humanity it has carried out, must act now. The UN Security Council, in particular, should take urgent measures to ensure the protection of civilians, provide for the unrestricted delivery of humanitarian assistance, and reverse ethnic cleansing in Darfur. It will soon be too late.

---

1. As of January 2006, delivering humanitarian assistance to Darfur remains difficult due to increased banditry and continued obstruction by the government of Sudan.

> "The American Government ... has consistently shown a disregard for international law and a contempt for human rights."

The United States Violates Human Rights Worldwide

Vernon Coleman

Americans claim to be champions of human rights, argues Vernon Coleman in the following viewpoint; however, he maintains, evidence of American human rights abuses and hypocrisy is widespread. For example, he asserts, the United States ignores human rights violations committed by its trading partners but carpet bombs the people of Iraq and Afghanistan. In addition, Coleman claims, Americans accuse others of war crimes but demand immunity for their own soldiers. Coleman is a physician, human and animal rights activist, and prolific author.

As you read, consider the following questions:

1. What evidence does Coleman provide to illustrate that the United States violates the human rights of its own people?

2. According to the author, what is hypocritical about the American definition of a terrorist?

3. Why does America refuse to ratify the Kyoto Treaty, in the author's view?

The American Government constantly says one thing and does another. It imposes standards on the rest of the world which it refuses to accept itself. It has consistently shown a disregard for international law and a contempt for human rights.

The Americans claim to be the fount of goodness but they refuse to do anything to help poor countries—indeed, over the last couple of decades they have introduced policies which have directly led to the deaths of millions of innocent people. America's idea of diplomacy is to carpet bomb countries which upset America.

The Americans deny basic human rights to whole countries and then arrogantly claim that they know best. They insist that price stability within America is more important than the future of the planet; they continue to destroy our environment (as well as their own) and to wage war against innocents all around the world.

American Hypocrisy

Virtually every day there are reports of American hypocrisy. The American president claims that his country leads the world in justice and yet his is one of the few countries which routinely executes children.[1] American presidents wage war to distract attention from their sexual peccadilloes. They insist that developing countries have properly supervised elections and yet they themselves conduct a presidential election which is decided when the so-called Supreme Court arbitrarily decides not to recount votes which would almost certainly have changed the result of the election.

1. In 2005 the U.S. Supreme Court ruled that the death penalty for minors was unconstitutional.

A headline in an American newspaper ran: 'All Nations on Earth Sign Global Warming Agreement. USA Refuses.' And still they wonder why everyone loathes and despises them.

Americans know little or nothing about other countries. Even their leading politicians have no idea where other countries are or who leads them. The Americans expect the rest of the world to worship their flag, but they seem unable to understand that respect has to be earned and cannot simply be demanded. The Americans believe that their definitions are the only ones that count; they believe that if they say that someone is a terrorist then the rest of the world must regard him as a terrorist. The Americans fund terrorists in Ireland but think that the English are being unreasonable if they complain. Within days of the September 11th [2001, terrorist] attack, the American Government decided to continue supporting Irish terrorists who were bombing innocent English targets.

The Americans believe that the only form of justice that matters is American justice—even though to the rest of the world American justice doesn't look, sound or smell much like justice at all.

A Commercial View of Human Rights

The Americans have a commercial view of human rights. They change their views according to the combatants. The Americans regard China as an important trading partner so they put up with human rights violations there. The Americans need Saudi oil so they turn a blind eye to human rights violations in that country too. But they will carpet bomb Afghanistan and Iraq to force regime changes in those countries.

The Americans claim to respect the freedom of the press and the individual's freedom of speech, but they will close down websites which are critical of America. When Americans closed down my website, the American FBI refused to cooperate with the British police to arrest the criminal involved. But when a British citizen interfered with American websites the Americans insisted that the British authorities deal with him.

In February 2003, at the same time that they were begging for British support for their latest war on Iraq, the Americans told the South Africans to arrest an innocent British pensioner but then left him in prison for ten days before even bothering to go and interview him.

There is, in American hearts and minds, one rule for Americans and one rule for the rest of the world. The Americans are widely loathed. And the loathing will get worse, much worse, before it gets better.

Americans claim to offer freedom on religious matters but insist that the world convert to Christianity—preferably of the right variety. The Americans regard themselves as missionaries—chosen by God to lead the world. And still they wonder why the world dislikes them.

To Americans, history started just after they stole their nation from the natives. There is no equality of opportunity in the USA but they pretend there is. The American revolution started with the battle-cry 'No taxation without representation'. But the Americans now tax the world—and refuse to allow any representation.

The Americans have handed power to the lobbyists and the public relations specialists. He who has the biggest bank balance has the most power. That is the American version of freedom. Frankly, it stinks.

A Global Distrust of America

It is hardly surprising that around the world people distrust America and Americans. It is hardly surprising that very few non-Americans have much confidence or faith in America.

The Americans steal, corrupt and pollute without a thought for the rest of the world. They are contemptuous and

Reproduced by permission of Copley News Service.

condescending, greedy and uncaring. They refuse to accept international laws on how to deal with prisoners of war. They demand immunity from the war crimes court for their own soldiers. They are by far the world's biggest polluter but they refuse to ratify the Kyoto Treaty because it may damage their own internal economy. They steal and patent seeds and plants and then sell those seeds and plants back to starving people in developing countries. They foist genetically engineered products on a world which doesn't want them. They claim to worship capitalism and freedom and yet the American government owns nearly 40% of all land in the USA.

The greed and dishonesty of corporate employees in America has been a primary factor in helping to push the world economy into recession. And still they wonder why the rest of the world dislikes them.

The Americans think they are disliked because they are rich. They are wrong. Very wrong. They are disliked, in part, because of the way they got rich and because of the way they now behave.

American Imperialism

But it is the belligerence and imperialsim of successive American governments which has really created world-wide hatred for America.

In recent years, America seems to have been forever invading, bombing or encouraging guerrillas—as long as they were right wing, of course. The Americans often manage to kill more of the wrong people or their allies (or both) than of the alleged enemy. Millions of innocents have died at the hands of the ruthless Americans. (Corporate America, however, invariably makes a profit out of war. Before attacking Iraq in 2003, the USA awarded American companies lucrative contracts to rebuild the country.)

A growing—and not inconsiderable—number of people around the world now sincerely believe that even if the American Government didn't actually plan the September 11th attack then they certainly knew about it beforehand. Why would they do such a terrible thing? The argument is a simple one. The September 11th attack has given the American Government an excellent excuse for removing freedom from its own people and for beginning an eternal war against the rest of the world.

Ever since September 11th, the Americans, followed faithfully by the British and the rest of the EU [European Union], have been making new laws faster than even the lawyers can keep up with them. There are now laws that even lawyers don't know about. In tomorrow's new world everyone will be a criminal. It will be all too easy for a Government to arrest any citizen who is regarded as a troublemaker.

It is hardly surprising that the world now hates America.

> "[The U.N.] Commission [on Human Rights] is almost unable to 'name and shame' even the most despotic governments."

Rogue Nations Undermine the United Nations' Mission to Promote Human Rights

Joseph Loconte

In the following viewpoint Joseph Loconte claims that allowing rogue nations to serve on the United Nations Commission on Human Rights undermines its efforts to address human rights violations. According to Loconte, several repressive regimes sit on the commission, including China, known for its oppression of political and religious groups, and Sudan, guilty of genocide. These countries, Loconte argues, thwart efforts to adopt effective resolutions to stop human rights abuses. Loconte is the William E. Simon Fellow in Religion and a Free Society at the Heritage Foundation, a conservative think tank in Washington, D.C.

As you read, consider the following questions:

Joseph Loconte, "Human Rights and Wrongs," *Weekly Standard*, vol. 9, p. 19. March 22, 2004. Reproduced by permission.

1. Why was the United Nations so eager to support the Universal Declaration of Human Rights, in Loconte's view?

2. According to the author, why will the United States be playing both offense and defense on the commission?

3. Why did Charles Malik question whether democratic nations would have the resolve to implement the Universal Declaration of Human Rights, according to Loconte?

The United Nations [U.N.] Commission on Human Rights begins its 60th session [in March 2004] . . . in Geneva. For . . . six weeks the 53 member states will generate, if nothing else, a cacophony of moral indignation.

Delegates will hear about the use of torture in Iran, violence against women in Saudi Arabia, and the abduction of children by militias across Africa. Burma may finally come in for a scolding, after years of military atrocities. Israel, as usual, will face numerous resolutions condemning its treatment of Palestinians, though none is likely to criticize [Palestinian leader] Yasser Arafat [who died on November 11, 2004]. The United States can expect bitter denunciations for its war on terrorism, while state sponsors of Islamic jihadists may escape blame. The [George W.] Bush administration will be working, meanwhile, to advance a new coalition of democracies intended to outmaneuver the dictatorships.

A Rogue's Gallery

The Commission's byzantine deliberations, then, will resemble those of the U.N. General Assembly—awash in both high-mindedness and hypocrisy. "What you'll see is how effective and skilled the dictatorships are in the diplomatic game," says Michael Goldfarb, press officer for Freedom House, the oldest human rights organization in the world. "They've turned the Commission into a rogues' gallery and effectively killed any substantive debate about human rights."

U.N. officials reject that view, but recent history tends to support it. State Department officials point to at least 18 repressive regimes now on the Commission, whose members serve three-year terms. China exerts strong influence, despite the Communist government's unrelenting crackdowns on political and religious groups. Nigeria, another member, is widely reported to support torture, extrajudicial killings, and radical Islam. Sudan is guilty of genocide and considered a state sponsor of terrorism. The Commission has no agreed definition of terrorism; it even endorsed suicide bombings against Israel as a legitimate form of armed conflict. In a 2001 vote that stunned the Bush administration, the Commission expelled the United States, a first in the body's history. Libya held the chair [in 2003], elected by a vote of 33 to 3.

The upshot is that the Commission is almost unable to "name and shame" even the most despotic governments. Take North Korea. Evidence had mounted for years of its brutalities—state-backed torture, starvation, death camps—yet no resolution condemning it was passed until [2003]. "The Human Rights Commission has taken many years to get to the sad place that it is today," says Lome Kraner, assistant secretary of state for democracy, human rights, and labor. "If you don't want to be criticized by the Commission, the best thing to do is to get a seat on the Commission."

A Universal Declaration of Human Rights

That's a far cry from the ideals laid out in the Universal Declaration of Human Rights, the seminal document of the original Commission on Human Rights created after World War II. With the atrocities of the Holocaust still fresh, the authors warned that "disregard and contempt for human rights have resulted in barbarous acts which have outraged the conscience of mankind." The Declaration's 30 articles enumerate political and social rights, including the right to life and liberty, equality under the law, and freedom of speech and assembly. There are also prohibitions against slavery, torture, and arbitrary arrest.

The crown jewel is Article 18: the right to freedom of thought, conscience, and religion. The provision, drafted by Lebanese ambassador Charles Malik, includes the right to change one's religion. When first proposed, it enraged the Communist and Muslim delegates (six of the original European members belonged to the Soviet bloc, while nine members claimed Islam as their dominant religion). Nevertheless, Malik—an Arab Christian and a powerful intellectual force on the Commission—stood his ground. "All those who stress the elemental economic rights and needs of man are for the most part impressed by his sheer animal existence. This is materialism, whatever else it may be called," Malik argued. "But unless men's proper nature, unless his mind and spirit are brought out, set apart, protected, and promoted, the struggle for human rights is a sham and a mockery."

The U.N. General Assembly adopted the Declaration in 1948 without a single dissenting vote (though with a number of states abstaining). Its language affirming the "equal and inalienable rights" of all people influenced scores of postwar and postcolonial constitutions and treaties. Drew University's Johannes Morsink calls it the "secular bible" for literally hundreds of advocacy groups and thousands of foot soldiers in the field.

Inevitably, though, the Declaration is widely referenced but little understood. Its social and economic guarantees—which include even a "right to rest and leisure"—are regularly invoked to deflect attention from violations of more fundamental rights.

Playing Offense and Defense

That may be changing. The Bush administration regards the promotion of democratic freedoms as essential to the war on

Cartoon by Chuck Asay, 2001. Reproduced by permission of Creators Syndicate.

terrorism. "As long as the Middle East remains a place where freedom does not flourish," Bush said [in 2003] "it will remain a place of stagnation, resentment, and violence ready for export." In a policy speech [in March 2004] Secretary of State Colin Powell said the United States would "always keep in the forefront of our efforts the necessity to deal with human rights in every country that we have relations with."

What might this mean in Geneva? The United States, back on the Commission, is expected to push for statements or resolutions on Belarus, Burma, Cuba, Iran, Nepal, Nigeria, North Korea, and Zimbabwe. Richard Williamson, chairman of the U.S. delegation, wants a resolution against China, but acknowledges it will be difficult to pass. This despite Beijing's record of arbitrary arrests, prison camps, and "egregious violations" against religious communities, according to Human Rights Watch and other groups. As David Aikman, author of *Jesus in Beijing*, told Congress ... "China's political leadership appears to have decided that any religion in China, if not strictly supervised, could turn into the regime's Achilles' heel."

The administration also will have to play defense. A Brazilian resolution defeated [in 2003] is expected to be recycled, calling for a ban on all forms of discrimination by sexual orientation. Conservative groups see this as a ploy to marginalize religious organizations that uphold traditional marriage—an effort already gaining ground in Europe. ([In 2003] Sweden criminalized speech that might be "offensive or threatening" to homosexuals, and charges already have been brought against a Pentecostal pastor.) Moreover, the resolution does not define sexual orientation or limit sexual "rights" by age, which could make it more difficult to prevent the abuse and trafficking of children.

Thwarting Resolutions

Commission watchers say that until its membership improves, its work will be seriously compromised. The problem is not only rogue governments, but regional coalitions that help elect states to terms on the Commission and then work to thwart resolutions against them. Even the democracies in Africa, for example, tend to overlook brutalities committed by their neighbors. Mark Lagon, deputy assistant secretary of state at the Bureau of International Organization Affairs, suggests that nations under U.N. sanctions not be allowed on the Commission. Meanwhile, foreign ministers from 10 democracies— including Chile, Poland, South Korea, and the United States— are promoting a Community of Democracies to function as a caucus within the United Nations. Members must actually adhere to the principles of the U.N. Charter and the Universal Declaration of Human Rights. During the session in Geneva, they plan to build support for a resolution promoting democratic institutions.

U.N. officials deny the suggestion that the human rights commission has betrayed its founding vision, or that higher standards for participation are needed. "You don't advance human rights by preaching only to the converted," argues Shashi Tharoor, U.N. undersecretary-general for communications and public information. "The ship of universal human rights cannot set sail by leaving human beings from some countries on the shore."

Others disagree. Habib Malik, son of Charles Malik and a professor at the Lebanese American University in Beirut, explains that those suffering under repressive regimes won't be rescued by the anemic values of multiculturalism. "The argument that 'inclusiveness' is the only way these states may start to change—I think it's baloney," he says. "You have to emphasize the practical and empirical power of a set of moral directives . . . to uphold individual rights."

It may be that the Universal Declaration has been more useful to that end than the Commission—just as Charles Malik seems to have anticipated. Even as the Commission was working to win approval of the Universal Declaration (no small feat at the onset of the Cold War), he wondered whether democratic nations would have the resolve to implement its principles. "I have observed a certain degree of inordinate caution, nay perhaps even of cynicism, with regard to carrying out the mandate," Malik said. "It is as though the real will to achieve and ensure human rights were lacking." The passage of time has borne out his lament.

> *"What we see across the Middle East is an expansion not of democracy but of occupation."*

U.S. Invasions Have Not Spread Democracy in the Middle East

Phyllis Bennis

Claims by the George W. Bush administration that the invasion of Iraq is spreading democracy in the Middle East are misguided, argues Phyllis Bennis in the following viewpoint. What Americans see as signs of democracy, she maintains, are simply efforts by dictatorial regimes to appease the United States. If power remains in the hands of dictators and absolute monarchs, she asserts, elections in the Middle East are meaningless. Bennis is an activist on issues concerning the Middle East and author of Before and After: U.S. Foreign Policy and the September 11th Crisis.

As you read, consider the following questions:

1. According to Bennis, what Lebanese protesters did the Bush administration choose to ignore?

Phyllis Bennis, "Democracy or Occupation: What's Really on the Rise Across the Middle East?" *Institute for Policy Studies*, March 12, 2005. Reproduced by permission.

2. Why did anti-Syrian protesters model their protest after the "Orange Revolution" in Ukraine, in the author's opinion?

3. How does the author describe the first Palestinian intifada?

In a recent broadcast of "Democracy Now," the well-known Egyptian feminist, novelist and activist Nawal al-Sadawi put it exactly right. Responding to President Bush's bragging that his policies, specifically his invasion and occupation of Iraq, were somehow responsible for the new moves towards "democracy" across the Middle East, she said, "This is a new kind of imperialism. Now they don't only steal our land and our resources, but they steal our struggles as well."

Misunderstanding Middle Eastern Democracy

There is indeed a moment of opportunity underway in a number of countries across the Middle East. It may turn out to be a truly historical moment. But if it does, it will be because people across the region have been fighting for their rights, for their freedom, for their own democracy, for many years. The claim that George Bush and the invasion of Iraq have brought about a sudden explosion of democracy, an "unexpected whiff of freedom" as the *New York Times* put it, is simply specious. It is insulting to the decades-long struggle of Palestinian, Iraqi, Egyptian, Lebanese, Syrian and other activists. It attempts to equate military occupation by the U.S. and its allies with democracy, and the struggle against those occupations with terrorism. And it stands in defiance of history.

In November 2003, speaking at the Cold War-era and ideologically grounded National Endowment for Democracy, Bush said that "accommodating the lack of freedom in the Middle East did nothing to make us safe." It was a classic Bushism—both because he had no intention of changing the reality of that accommodationism beyond new rhetoric, and because his understanding of and valuation of Middle Eastern democracy started and stopped with its impact on the United States.

It is no secret that U.S. support for absolute monarchies and dictatorial regimes disguised as 'democracies' across the Middle East has been and remains the linchpin of those regimes' ability to remain in power. In the past that support was justified on the basis of maintaining U.S. control of crucial oil production, and maintaining U.S. strategic/military domination of the vital region. Now Bush implies that those days may be over. But without any effort to diminish global reliance on Middle Eastern oil and thus U.S. determination to control the world's access to that oil, the claim falls flat.

Urging Egypt's [President] Hosni Mubarak to release from jail the leader of a small pro-U.S. party is easy. But until we see the $2 billion annual U.S. aid to Egypt held back conditional on the massive opening of Egypt's political and economic system, there is no basis to take seriously the claim that the White House is supporting Egyptian democracy. Applauding Palestinian elections is easy. But until the U.S. is prepared to bring about the real empowerment of Palestinian democracy by ending the military occupation of their land through withholding economic, military, political, and diplomatic aid to Israel until it ends the occupation of all of the West Bank, Gaza and East Jerusalem, there is no basis to take seriously Bush's claim to support democracy in a viable Palestinian state.

Selected Images of Democracy

Bush and his minions pointed over and over again at the media-friendly images of thousands of western-style Lebanese demonstrators filling Beirut's Martyrs' Square complete with midriff-baring t-shirts and ubiquitous cell phones. They were calling for an end to Syrian occupation of Lebanon, for the

14,000 Syrian troops and 5,000 or so Syrian intelligence operatives to go home. But when far more demonstrators, somewhere between half a million and a million Lebanese took over downtown Beirut in a different demonstration, spilling out of Martyrs' Square to fill the surrounding streets of the capital, calling for an end to ALL foreign interference and for Syria to go home as determined by Beirut and Damascus and not by Washington, the White House had nothing to say. These Lebanese demonstrators were not the ones to whom Bush promised that "when you stand for freedom we will stand with you." There were few cell phones and far fewer tight t-shirts among them; these Lebanese were traditional and, more crucially, largely poor. Unlike at least some of the anti-Syria protesters, this group did not and does not look to the U.S. as their strategic partner.

The anti-Syrian mobilization of protesters in Beirut reflected an overwhelmingly middle- and upper-class strata of mostly young urban Lebanese. As noted by Lebanese University sociologist Ahmed Beydoun, they "want their institutions to work normally, which is prevented by Syrian influence. It is not a problem with the political system itself." That means they want the existing political system to work better—not to transform that system. They want elections free of Syrian domination, but still based on the existing confessional system that has controlled Lebanon's politics since the French departed in 1932. It was based on an understanding that the parliament would have a six-to-five Christian majority, and continues to dole out political positions based on the 1932 census. The president is a Maronite Christian, prime minister a Sunni, speaker of the parliament a Shi'a, etc. The population has changed dramatically but no census has been held since— and the anti-Syrian protesters are not calling for one, nor are they demanding elections based on a one-person-one-vote system instead of one controlled by sectarian power.

An Unexpected Model

Lebanon's increase in anti-Syrian protests followed the assassination of the former prime minister, Rafik Hariri, which the U.S., despite the lack of evidence, blamed on Syria. It was notable that the anti-Syrian protesters themselves wore orange and claimed that their model was the recent "Orange Revolution" movement that helped topple the government of Ukraine—not the recent U.S.-controlled elections in Iraq. Those parallels are telling—in Ukraine, too, the mass mobilizations supported Viktor Yushchenko, a leader known, as was Hariri, for his pro-Western, pro-globalization, explicitly pro-U.S. views. New information confirming that U.S. doctors had to work in secret to help diagnose and treat Yuschenko's dioxin poisoning, provides some indication of how damaging those U.S. links might have proved for his campaign if they had been made public.

It was not surprising that Bush paid little attention to the much larger group of [pro-Syrian] Lebanese demonstrators who did not play the role of extras in a White House-orchestrated extravaganza. After all, how often has the Bush administration paid attention to huge demonstrations within the U.S. itself, calling protesters in the streets of Washington or New York "heroes of democracy?" His approach continues the selective use of images trotted out or carefully ignored by the Bush administration to bolster its claim of "bringing democracy to the Middle East." . . .

Elections Under Occupation

The U.S. appropriation of Arab democratic yearnings spread far beyond Lebanon. Palestinians held relatively free and fair elections in January [2005]! They elected a moderate leader eager to engage with the U.S.! Of course it was possible only because 150,000 U.S. troops were occupying Iraq and planning to give the Iraqis elections! Ignored, of course, was that these elections, held under conditions of a 37-year-old mili-

Valuing Obedience over Democracy

The US has been the main supporter of dictatorships in the Mideast for the last fifty years. It has backed the Shah of Iran, the Saudi Monarchy, Egypt's dictatorship, [Iraq's] Saddam Hussein himself, and of course the Israeli occupation of Palestine. A leopard does not change its spots. The US cares nothing for democracy; it supports regimes that agree to its terms and overthrows those that disagree whether they are democratic or autocratic. The US values obedience not democracy.

Ashley Smith,
Counterpunch, *March 23, 2005.*

tary occupation, provided a framework of democracy for a people still denied the power to use it. Ignored, as well, was the long and often bitter struggle of Palestinians for both democracy and freedom. Ignored, too, was the election of 1996, in which Yasir Arafat was elected not with the 99% vote so typical of Egypt and other U.S. allies, but by a strong but not overwhelming majority of 68% or so.

Much of the U.S. jubilation over the Palestinian elections was not with the "free and fair" nature of the vote, a difficult assessment under military occupation, but rather with the results. The choice of Mahmoud Abbas, or Abu Mazen, reflected a political situation parallel in certain ways to the 1990 Nicaraguan election that ousted the Sandinista government in favor of the U.S.-backed Violeta Chamorro. After more than a decade of the U.S.-backed contra war against the Sandinista government, the Nicaraguan population was told explicitly that if they voted the Sandinistas back in, the U.S. would continue to impose war, famine, and economic collapse. Only a vote for Chamorro, Nicaraguans were told, offered a chance to rebuild ties with the U.S. and reconstruct the country. What a surprise Chamorro won overwhelmingly. Similarly, while Abu Mazen maintained the legitimate credential of having been the close confidant of the revered late Yasir Arafat, he did not have an independent political base and instead gained a great deal from public awareness that he was the only candidate with whom Israel and the U.S. were prepared to negotiate.

Mobilizing Against Occupation

Palestinian democracy overall is more advanced than in much of the region, reflecting the advances in Palestinian civil society built on mobilization against the occupation. As a result Abu Mazen's election was by a margin of something close to 60%, with 20% for the human rights campaign [of] Mustafa Barghouti and another 20% divided among other candidates. Much of the history of Palestinian democracy remains unknown even within the Arab world. The *New York Times* quoted a Lebanese anti-Syrian demonstrator applauding her demonstration as "something unknown for the Arab world—it is pacifist, it is democratic and it is spontaneous," she said. Her statement betrayed a lack of familiarity not only with the Palestinian elections, but far more important, the legacy of the first Palestinian intifada, or uprising, from 1987 to 1993. That mobilization was unarmed; it was symbolized internationally by children with stones, but without any actual weapons or suicide bombings. The intifada spontaneously generated popular movements to empower women and young people, to guard villages from Israeli soldiers' incursions, to grow and distribute food during long curfews, to provide medical assistance to villages and refugee camp residents unable to travel to hospitals, to organize workers to defend their rights, to build tax resistance and other non-violent protest activities, and to mobilize the entire society against the occupation. The uprising created, during those six years, a new Palestinian culture far more democratic than anything that had existed before. The success of Palestinian election efforts in the current, post-Oslo period [of Palestinian-Israeli peace talks] is rooted in that earlier intifada democracy.

Democracy in Egypt

Then there's Egypt. Hosni Mubarak has "won" four six-year terms as president since he took over from the assassinated Anwar Sadat, with polls running in the high 90% brackets every time. A close ally of the U.S., every administration since that of Jimmy Carter has maintained massive economic aid to Egypt, and welcomed it as a strategic and "democratic" ally. . . . Following gentle verbal prodding by Bush, [secretary of state Condoleezza] Rice and others but no change in actual U.S. support, Mubarak announced that for the first time other candidates would be allowed to run for president. The shift has been trumpeted as part of Bush's "new freedom" spreading across the Middle East.

Certainly there is a shifting moment of history underway in the region, including in Egypt. But that moment has been created largely by the political motion of sometimes outlawed or semi-legal parties, human rights organizations, trade unions, students' and lawyers' associations, women's mobilizations, and many other parts of civil society continuing to work despite repression over years and decades and generations.

A more sober and cautious view of what has and has not changed in Egypt would provide a different assessment than the Egypt-is-becoming-democratic-because-we-invaded-Iraq claims of the Bush administration. Mubarak continues to rule under the terms of an emergency law in place since 1981 that gives the president virtually unchallengeable power. He has made clear that only parties accepted as legitimate by the current Mubarak-dominated parliament will be allowed to run for office. The Muslim Brotherhood, the largest, one of the oldest and most influential Islamist parties, remains outlawed.

The Kifaya ("Enough") movement has held demonstrations calling on Mubarak to step down from the presidency and to refrain from handing over his presidency to his son Gamal, widely viewed as his chosen heir apparent. The movement is functioning, but it is unclear whether it will be allowed to field a candidate for president.

Pro-globalization, Not Democracy

The Ghad ("Tomorrow") party is the favored party of the Bush administration and the U.S. press. Egyptian authorities arrested Ghad leader Ayman Nour [in 2005], and the U.S. responded harshly, demanding that he be released. Secretary of State Condoleezza Rice even postponed a planned Egyptian trip to protest Nour's arrest. He was released on March 12 [2005]. But Washington's support for Ghad is rooted less in real opposition to Mubarak's repressive government, than in recognition of the party's overall pro-globalization, pro-privatization and pro-U.S. stance. Although Nour made a name for himself providing social services to poor Cairenes, his party's human rights focus is largely limited to political rights, not economic and social rights, and it does not have a long-time or wide-spread level of support among the Egyptian population.

The political climate in Egypt has also been transformed in recent years, despite continuing repression and the government's refusal to open the political system, by the work of human rights organizations. Many have criticized the arbitrary round-ups, particularly of Islamist organizations, and most especially in the period since the October 2004 bombings in the Egyptian resort town of Taba.

Trade union and other workers' organizations have initiated strikes protesting the pro-business, pro-globalization, anti-worker policies of Mubarak, and particularly of his son Gamal. In February 2005 there was a large strike against the campaign to privatize a large nationalized company.

Is Democracy Really on the Rise?

As the *Christian Science Monitor* noted on February 28, [2005,] "most of the recent shifts toward democracy have been top-down initiatives by regimes eager to appease Washington." There is a long history in the Middle East of repressive regimes making minor concession designed to appease equally symbolic demands of Washington, only to withdraw the new privilege when American eyes have turned away. The Kuwaiti royals' post-Desert Storm promises of democratization never materialized. The Saudi municipal council "elections" recently held were designed to pacify U.S. concerns; but with only men allowed to vote at all, and half the council members still chosen by the royal family, little power changed hands.

At the end of the day, what we see across the Middle East is an expansion not of democracy but of occupation. Israel "allowed" the Palestinians to hold elections (despite consistent harassment, arrests, detentions of all candidates other than Israel's favorite) but the occupation remains unchecked, and settlement-expansion and the Wall continue to seize and hold increasing tracts of West Bank and East Jerusalem land. The U.S., under pressure from Ayatollah Ali al-Sistani, finally agreed to hold elections in occupied Iraq, but the military occupation and its deadly consequences, including dozens of Iraqis killed on a daily basis, continues.

If the reality of occupation is to be equated with the false claim of democracy, is the false prize worth the all-too-real price?

Periodical Bibliography

The following articles have been selected to supplement the diverse views presented in this chapter.

Jasper Becker	"It's Time to Disengage with Kim Jong Il," *Time*, February 14, 2005.
Christianity Today	"Nightmares and Miracles," December 2004.
Nicholas Eberstadt	"Tear Down This Tyranny," *Weekly Standard*, November 29, 2004.
Economist	"Much Abused: More Evidence, but Little Action," November 27, 2004.
Julie Flint	"Quiet Diplomacy Will Not Save Darfur," *Independent*, August 30, 2004.
Roya Johnson	"Defeating Misogyny in Iran," *American Thinker*, April 5, 2005.
Jacqueline M. Massey	"A Nobel Cause," *Herizons*, Fall 2004.
Ronald J. McNamara	"Iran Human Rights in Crisis," *American Chronicle*, August 12, 2005.
Thomas Omestad	"Focusing on Human Rights," *Nieman Reports*, Fall 2004.
Thomas Omestad	"Gulag Nation," *U.S. News & World Report*, June 23, 2004.
Eric Reeves	"Genocide in Sudan," *In These Times*, May 6, 2004.
Henry Rosemont	"Executing Human Rights: The United States Versus the United Nations," *Resist*, January 2000.
Robert Scheer	"Human Rights, Rendered Meaningless," *San Francisco Chronicle*, December 14, 2005.

OPPOSING
VIEWPOINTS®
SERIES

CHAPTER 4

How Should the Global Community Respond to Rogue Nations?

Chapter Preface

Fifty-one nations signed the United Nations (UN) charter on October 24, 1945, thereby establishing this international peace-keeping organization. The UN's primary goal was to save succeeding generations from the scourge of war, to promote human rights, and to encourage respect for international law and treaties. After the United States and Great Britain invaded Iraq without UN approval in March 2003, the UN Security Council, charged with maintaining peace and security among nations, became bitterly divided, and some commentators have begun to question whether the UN can protect global security. "The major centers of power either act unilaterally or within the context of regional alliances like NATO [North Atlantic Treaty Organization]—not the U.N.," claims foreign policy analyst Daniel Goure. "When it comes to the U.N. and issues of security," he asserts, "the world is moving on." Many analysts agree that the manner in which the UN responds to rogue nations will determine whether the organization can live up to its mandate.

Few nations have confidence that the UN can effectively protect its members against the threat posed by rogue nations. Foreign policy expert Nile Gardiner maintains, "A lot hinges on how the U.N. handles the biggest security concerns we're facing right now: namely Iran and North Korea." If the U.N. were to disarm these nations, he argues, the institution could restore its credibility. "But if there is more inaction and appeasement," he asserts, "then the organization will be written off. And, given the bipolar power structure at the Security Council—with the U.S. and Britain on one side and France and Russia on the other—I really don't see any strong response from the U.N. on this issue any time soon," he concludes. To remain relevant, critics argue, the UN must redraft its charter. The charter's critics claim that Article 51, which allows nations to defend themselves if attacked, is an anachronism in an age when rogue nations with weapons of mass destruction could kill millions instantaneously. "We are now living in an age of international terrorism and rogue states," Gardiner maintains, "but that's not reflected in Article 51." Goure agrees, adding that countries should be allowed to take "anticipatory self-defense" actions against rogue nations. "This needs to be written simply and directly" into the U.N. charter, Goure maintains.

Columbia University political science professor Tom Weiss disagrees. He contends that Article 51 has evolved to encompass the threat posed by rogue nations. "No one, not even international lawyers, dispute the fact the Article 51 now gives you a right to pre-emptively defend yourself if you're threatened," he avers. Foreign policy scholar Christopher Preble agrees, adding, "The United Nations wouldn't have opposed [U.S.] intervention in Iraq if the majority of member states believed that Iraq was a threat to the U.S. That was the problem: they didn't believe that we were genuinely threatened." Indeed, UN expert Bill Durch maintains that the Security Council had no qualms about authorizing American action against Afghanistan after the terrorist attacks of September 11, 2001 (as many of the terrorists had trained in Afghanistan). "It came under the purview of Article 51 and was fine, because, in this case, the United States had legitimately been threatened."

Commentators continue to debate whether the United Nations can effectively respond to the threat posed by rogue nations. The authors in the following chapter debate the effectiveness of other responses to today's global insecurities.

> "When the best intelligence we have, plus the nature of the beast, counsels force, then we must use it."

Preemptive Force Is Sometimes Necessary to Contain Rogue Nations

National Review

The United States and its allies cannot depend on intelligence agencies alone to determine whether rogue nations have developed weapons of mass destruction, argue the editors of National Review, *a journal of conservative political opinion. U.S. leaders should trust their suspicions that secretive, dictatorial regimes that hate the United States pose a serious national security threat. Indeed, the authors maintain, the United States should be prepared to use preemptive force to contain these dangerous rogue states.*

As you read, consider the following questions:

1. According to the editors of *National Review*, how were the intelligence community and the Bush administration pressured by their own expectations?

National Review, "Intelligence Quotient," February 23, 2004. Reproduced by permission.

2. In addition to preemption, what strategies in dealing with rogue nations do the authors recommend?

3. How must the case for preemption be made to the public, in the authors' view?

"It turns out we were all wrong" about [former Iraqi president] Saddam Hussein's WMD [weapons of mass destruction], former chief weapons inspector David Kay told the Senate Armed Services Committee. These blunt words, after months of failing to find such weapons, forced President [George W.] Bush to call for a bipartisan commission to examine American intelligence operations.

Kay repudiated a central article of faith in the religion of conspiracy: that the administration, hot to topple Saddam, pressured intelligence analysts to give it the evidence it needed. Kay said he had "not come across a single one" who had been leaned on in that fashion. The intelligence community and the administration alike were, however, pressured by their own expectations. Saddam had possessed and used poison gas, and was determined to build other forms of WMD. He had been defying U.N. inspectors for four years. Therefore, it seemed likely that he had restocked his arsenal. The Bush administration believed it; so did the [Bill] Clinton administration. So did Britain. So did the anti-war Left, including France and Germany. (One reason the peaceniks advanced for not invading Iraq was that Saddam would unleash his WMD.)

Learning from an Intelligence Failure

Expectations cut both ways. We presumed that Libya was too low-tech to have a serious nuclear program—until Colonel [Muammar] Qaddafi [Libya's leader] told us that he would abandon one that was more advanced than we had imagined. Intelligence agencies must be able to stretch their own paradigms, to cast a wide net. Clearly ours, which have enjoyed a long romance with technological data-gathering at the expense of human intelligence, need a shake-up.

The Doctrine of Preemption

We must adapt the concept of imminent threat to the capabilities and objectives of today's adversaries. Rogue states and terrorists do not seek to attack us using conventional means. They know such attacks would fail. Instead, they rely on acts of terror and, potentially, the use of weapons of mass destruction—weapons that can be easily concealed, delivered covertly, and used without warning. . . .

The United States has long maintained the option of preemptive actions to counter a sufficient threat to our national security. The greater the threat, the greater is the risk of inaction—and the more compelling the case for taking anticipatory action to defend ourselves, even if uncertainty remains as to the time and place of the enemy's attack. To forestall or prevent such hostile acts by our adversaries, the United States will, if necessary, act preemptively.

Office of the White House,
"The National Security Strategy of the United States of America,"
September 2002.

But intelligence can never tell us everything. Leaders must understand the minds of their enemies, and the nature of the world they live in. Furtive, dictatorial, aggressive regimes with powerful grudges against the United States deserve our suspicion. When they are patrons of terror, they deserve our hostility. [The terrorist attack of] September 11—which was accomplished not by WMD, but by box cutters—has raised the stakes immeasurably. Such countries as North Korea, Iran, Libya, and Saddam's Iraq must understand that they live on borrowed time. In many situations we will use diplomacy, as we have with North Korea and Libya. In others, we will wait on domestic developments, as in Iran. In still others, we will try isolation, as we did for many years with Iraq. But when the best intelligence we have, plus the nature of the beast, counsels force, then we must use it. We cannot wait, as [secretary of state] Condi Rice once put it, until our smoking gun is Chicago.

The administration must not think, however, that everyone understands and accepts pre-emption in an age of terror. These are new presumptions for a world that we now understand to be dangerous. The case for them must be made, and defended. It must also be accompanied by an assurance to the public that the intelligence gathering that assists our leaders in analyzing the threats against us will be done in the most intelligent way possible. The administration's insistence, until [February 21, 2004], that no mistakes had been made has not served it well.

"Aggressive U.S. military actions around the world merely motivate thuggish regimes to redouble their efforts to get super weapons faster."

Preemptive Force Threatens Efforts to Contain Rogue States

Ivan Eland

According to Ivan Eland in the following viewpoint, the George W. Bush administration's belief that the invasion of Iraq would scare rogue nations into discontinuing their pursuit of weapons of mass destruction (WMD) has backfired. This policy is almost certain to have the opposite effect, Eland asserts. Although Syria and Iran appear to be cooperating with the United States, they have in reality stepped up their efforts to obtain WMD, he maintains. Eland, a senior fellow at the Independent Institute, is author of Putting "Defense" Back into U.S. Defense Policy.

As you read, consider the following questions:

1. In what ways, according to Eland, has U.S. treatment of Iraq and North Korea differed?

Ivan Eland, "Look to Iran for the Real Costs of the War in Iraq," Independent Institute, May 9, 2003. Reproduced by permission of the Independent Institute, www.independent .org.

163

2. According to the author, how has the intimidation strategy against rogue states backfired in the past?

3. What does the author claim will probably deter rogue nations from attacking the United States?

The Bush administration is apparently astonished and concerned to learn that Iran has hastened its drive to get nuclear weapons. Would an American military presence in neighboring nations on two sides of that country—in Iraq and Afghanistan—have anything to do with that acceleration?

Countries like Iran (and Libya, Syria and the many other nations seeking weapons of mass destruction) noted that the United States invaded Iraq—a nation without nuclear weapons—but treated North Korea—a nation that went out of its way to inform the United States about its possession of nuclear weapons—much more gingerly. If you were an Iranian leader, what would you do?

The Real Response to the Invasion of Iraq

Perhaps the main reason the neo-conservatives, both inside and outside the Bush administration, pressed for an invasion of Iraq was to achieve a "demonstration effect." Their thinking was that other rogue nations (Syria and Iran in particular) would be intimidated and improve their behavior.

On the surface, there are some signs of increased cooperation with the United States on the part of Iran (helping out in Afghanistan and offering to assist with any downed American aircraft in the recent war with Iraq) and Syria (pledges to close the offices of anti-Israeli groups). But in secret, those nations are most likely racing as fast as they can to obtain weapons of mass destruction—to keep the United States from doing to them what it did to Saddam Hussein's regime [in Iraq].

The apparent acceleration of Iran's covert nuclear program proves that the Iraq war's intended demonstration effect has turned into a "proliferation effect."

President George W. Bush has said: "One of the things we must do is work together to stop the proliferation of weapons of mass destruction. It is a major issue that faces the world and it is an issue on which the United States will still lead."

Yet the administration's aggressive counter-proliferation policy of launching of "pre-emptive" attacks against states that are attempting to gain or possess weapons of mass destruction is backfiring. War on Iraq or not, proliferating nations know that U.S. public opinion will not support wars on the many countries that are developing or have such super weapons.

Before the Iraq War, the Pentagon noted that 10 nuclear programs, 13 countries with biological weapons, 16 nations with chemical weapons, and 28 countries with ballistic missiles were either existing or emerging threats to the United States and its allies. So chances are good that if countries conduct such programs in secret and bury or hide the facilities to secure them from U.S. air strikes, they can eventually obtain weapons whose technology is now fairly old.

Aggressive U.S. military actions around the world merely motivate thuggish regimes to redouble their efforts to get super weapons faster.

Learning from Libya

The intimidation strategy against rogue states has backfired in the past. The larger than life neo-conservative myth of their icon, President Ronald Reagan, dissuading Moammar Qaddafi of Libya from terrorist acts by bombing his tent is just that—a myth. After the 1986 air strikes on Libya, the historical record indicates that Qaddafi accelerated his terrorism but merely did it more covertly or contracted it out to independent terrorist groups.

The large number of Americans killed in the 1988 bombing of Pan Am flight 103 over Lockerbie, Scotland alone should have dispelled that myth. Similarly, intimidation will probably not curb fearful rogue states from trying to improve their

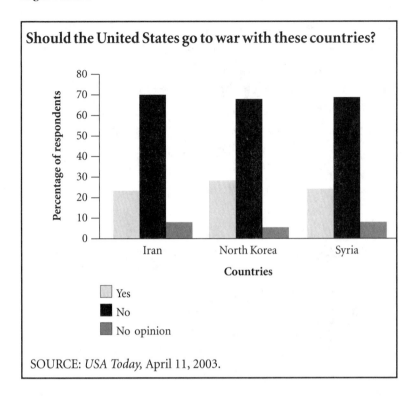

Should the United States go to war with these countries?

Countries

- Yes
- No
- No opinion

SOURCE: *USA Today,* April 11, 2003.

chances of survival by developing super weapons. Even though rogue states are despotic they do have legitimate fears of attacks by regional foes and now the United States.

Given the large number of nations that are working on weapons of mass destruction (particularly nuclear weapons), the United States may have to accept the unpleasant fact that some unsavory regimes might have them or get them. The good news is that most of those nations are poor and can afford no more than a few nuclear warheads. The bone-crushing dominance of the U.S. nuclear arsenal—with thousands of warheads—should be able to deter such countries from launching an attack on the United States.

Leaders from rogue nations are often portrayed in the American media as irrational and incapable of being deterred from attacks against the United States but have acquired, in their ascent to power in their own nations, the pragmatism of many politicians. In fact, if the United States refrained from unnecessary military interventions in the backwater regions of most of the rogue nations, those nations would have no cause to launch such weapons against the faraway United States in the first place.

But Bush has taken the opposite road of profligate and unneeded military interventions. The American public and media have basked in the glow of old glory being draped over the statue of Saddam in Iraq. But the unseemly downside of such American military adventurism may lie hidden in deeply buried bunkers in nations like Iran.

| "Focusing on the limited yet real threats posed by the 'rogues' is essential to making the case for missile defense."

A Missile Defense System Is Necessary to Protect Against Rogue Nations

Dennis Ross

Dennis Ross claims in the following viewpoint that despotic and unstable rogue regimes are less likely to be deterred by the threat of nuclear destruction than were the United States and the Soviet Union during the Cold War. Ross reasons that the United States and other major nuclear powers must therefore pursue missile defense programs that would destroy nuclear missiles launched by rogue states before these missiles reached their targets. Ross, a diplomat, is author of The Missing Peace: The Inside Story of the Fight for Middle East Peace.

As you read, consider the following questions:

1. According to Ross, what did President Reagan believe would facilitate strategic stability?

2. In the author's opinion, what message does modifying the Anti-Ballistic Treaty send to Russia?

Dennis Ross, "Rethinking Missile Defenses," *U.S. News & World Report*, April 2, 2001. Reproduced with permission.

3. What must the United States do to gain China's cooperation in missile defense, in the author's view?

As an old arms control negotiator, I saw the 1972 antiballistic missile treaty [ABM] as the linchpin of strategic stability. By limiting defenses, it reduced the incentive for either the United States or the former Soviet Union to continue the buildup of offensive missile forces. By introducing greater predictability into the Cold War equation, it diminished the risk of miscalculation. And, by reinforcing the reality of mutual vulnerability, it induced greater caution in crises.

Mutual Invulnerability

The logic of enshrining mutual vulnerability in a formal treaty had its share of critics. For former President Reagan, such logic was perverse. He believed that strategic stability would result from mutual invulnerability to attack, not mutual vulnerability. And he was convinced that it was possible to achieve mutual invulnerability through Star Wars—his strategic defense initiative (SDI).

For me, the issue was not the desirability but the feasibility of his concept. I saw no impenetrable shield, and I feared offensive technology would always outstrip defenses. Moreover, the costs were prohibitive, and the envisioned benefits did not warrant scrapping a framework that circumscribed defenses and paved the way for reducing offensive missile forces.

While Star Wars did not materialize, it probably did contribute to the Soviet Union's demise. Even if I questioned the feasibility of SDI, the Mikhail Gorbachev leadership did not. Arms control took on a new meaning for the Soviets, and so did reforming their system. But the steps Gorbachev took to reform his country and its system inevitably led to its undoing.

The Mission of National Missile Defense

The primary mission of National Missile Defense [NMD] is defense of the United States (all 50 states) against a threat of a limited strategic ballistic missile attack from a rogue nation. Such a system would also provide some capability against a small accidental or unauthorized launch of strategic ballistic missiles from more nuclear capable states. The means to accomplish the NMD mission are as follows:

- Field an NMD system that meets the ballistic missile threat at the time of a deployment decision.

- Detect the launch of enemy ballistic missile(s) and track.

- Continue tracking of ballistic missile(s) using ground based radars.

- Engage and destroy the ballistic missile warhead above the earth's atmosphere by force of impact.

Federation of American Scientists,
"National Missile Defense,"
July, 27, 2000. www.fas.org.

New Perils

The bipolarity of the Cold War disappeared, and with it the strategic world we had known. The ABM treaty helped to order that world and make it more predictable. But that world no longer exists, and in its place there are a small number of state actors motivated either by the megalomania of Saddam Hussein or by the revolutionary zeal and even the desire for martyrdom that exist in a part of the Iranian leadership. For them the use of weapons of mass destruction could serve a higher calling, even if it meant virtual destruction of their countries.

Defending ourselves against such threats is necessary, even if it requires the modification of the ABM treaty. Focusing on the limited yet real threats posed by the "rogues" is essential to making the case for missile defense. We clearly have problems with many of our European and Asian allies on missile defense. To bring our allies on board, we will have to show them the logic of it as well as a strategy for dealing with Russian and Chinese opposition to it. Our allies should be reminded of the relatively small but real threats we are all facing, the increasing feasibility of dealing with these threats, and the limited scope of missile defense we envision for ourselves and for them. They should see as well a good-faith effort to cooperate with the Russians and Chinese.

Accommodating Russian and Chinese Concerns

Neither Russia nor China has concerns that will be easy to accommodate. For the Russians, the ABM treaty stands as an emblem of their superpower status. Modifying it, in their eyes, sends a message that they are not the actors on the world stage that they once were. While we should not let the Russians prevent us from developing relevant missile defenses, we have a political interest in taking account of their concerns and in fostering their sense of inclusion in the development of these defenses.

There are several ways to do so. First, we should focus on promoting common assessments of possible threats from "rogue" states, something that should be of interest to the Russians given the proximity of these threats to Russia. Second, we should consider developing joint early-warning centers to deal with missile launches. Third, we should consider technological cooperation on theater missile defense, an area in which the Russians have done a lot of work and one that could be very important for our allies. If the Russians are prepared to cooperate, we should be prepared to broaden the scope of missile defense technology we share with them.

Such an approach might well diminish Russian opposition, but what about the Chinese? Their problem relates to Taiwan. They fear missile defenses will become a shield behind which those who favor Taiwan's independence can hide. Here we must be realistic, engaging the Chinese in a serious dialogue, emphasizing cooperation where possible, and reaffirming our "one China" policy. But they, too, must be realistic: There can be no solution to Taiwan that is based on coercion or the use of force.

In the end, it is in our interest to develop a limited missile defense. The pace of development should be set by the technology available and the emergence of real threats. Managing the politics of missile defense internationally requires working with our allies and providing a pathway for Russian involvement. While China may present a more formidable problem, missile defense is best handled as a part of our overall relationship—a relationship that is likely to be troubled for reasons other than our efforts to adjust the ABM treaty to a new strategic reality.

> *"This preposterous [rogue] 'threat' has been used for the past 10 years as a justification for continuing with the missile defence program."*

A Missile Defense System Is Unnecessary

Gwynne Dyer

The myth that rogue states pose a nuclear threat was created to justify the continued funding of costly missile defense technology, argues Gwynne Dyer in the following viewpoint. Even if these poor, technologically inferior nations were to develop nuclear weapons, claims Dyer, they would do so as a deterrent, not to launch an attack that would end in their own destruction. Nevertheless, Dyer maintains, Americans continue to spend tax dollars on a missile defense program that has yet to produce a successful interceptor missile. Dyer is a London-based independent international journalist.

As you read, consider the following questions:

1. According to Dyer, how did the Pentagon's Missile Defense Agency describe the goals of the December 2004 interceptor missile test?

Gwynne Dyer, "Shoot Down the 'Rogue States' Myth," *Spectator [Hamilton, Ontario]*, December 24, 2004. Reproduced by permission.

2. In the author's view, why is the timing of the creation of the new rogue threat significant?

3. What is the U.S. missile defense program really designed to defend against, in the author's opinion?

"We say to those tyrants who believe they can blackmail America and the free world: you fire, we're going to shoot it down," President George W. Bush told the voters of Ridley, Penn., on a campaign stop [in October 2004].

Many of his listeners probably believed him, since there is not a large reservoir of expertise on ballistic missile defence (BMD) in Ridley. But even they must have noticed that the interceptor missile he was boasting about failed yet again [in December 2004].

Ballistic Missile Defence Failures

It was the first full test in two years for the "ground-based midcourse" interceptor. None of the previous eight flight tests were conducted under realistic conditions and most of them failed anyway, so this time the Pentagon's Missile Defence Agency described the goal of the test in terms that precluded failure.

It was just going to be a "fly-by" of the incoming warhead (and nobody said how close). The interceptor missile managed to fail the test anyway: it didn't even get out of its silo.

The people of Ridley must be realizing around now that Bush's "we're going to shoot it down" remark was a trifle optimistic, but they probably still accept the bit about "the tyrants who believe they can blackmail America and the free world." They shouldn't. That is a myth that was created after the collapse of the Soviet Union, mostly for domestic political reasons.

The Rogue-State Myth

When the Soviet Union vanished at the start of the '90s, there was an urgent need for a new threat to justify the existing de-

Cartoon by Mike Keefe. Reproduced by permission of PoliticalCartoons.com.

fence budget, and if possible to persuade other countries that they still needed American protection. The think-tanks in Washington went to work on the problem, but all they could come up with was the so-called "rogue states."

The "rogue states"—the phrase first came into use in 1993–94—were countries that had nasty regimes and publicly defied the United States. Iraq, Iran and North Korea were always included on the list; Libya, Syria and Cuba sometimes got mentioned as well. They were poor, far away and technologically unimpressive, and there was no way they could actually hurt the United States, but at least they sounded hostile.

"Rogue states" were successfully sold to the U.S. public as a new threat that justified the old military forces and programs, but you couldn't really expect foreign governments to take them seriously. These were regimes that had already been in power for between 15 years (in Iran's case) and 40 years (in North Korea's).

Why had they suddenly become a mortal danger now, just after the Soviet threat disappeared? Why would they be crazy enough to attack the United States, even if they could?

Washington made much of the suspicion that Iran, North Korea and even Iraq were working on nuclear weapons, as though that would prove their evil intentions, but nobody else saw it that way. If they actually were seeking nuclear weapons, it would obviously be for deterrent purposes, since they all lived under the permanent threat of either Israeli or American nuclear attack.

A limited capability to strike back, even if only locally and only with a couple of warheads, would make them feel a lot safer.

Nobody else wanted Iran, Iraq or North Korea to have nuclear weapons, but they didn't see any likelihood of these countries developing intercontinental ballistic missiles. In any case, they simply did not believe that any of these regimes would deliberately commit suicide by firing a couple of missiles at the United States. They were nasty, but they weren't crazy.

A Justification for Missile Defence

In the United States, however, this preposterous "threat" has been used for the past 10 years as a justification for continuing with the missile defence program that [former U.S. president] Ronald Reagan may have believed would stop Soviet missiles. And it's really still about developing the ability to stop Russian and/or Chinese missiles in some future where the great powers have slid into a military confrontation once more.

The BMD system being deployed now probably couldn't stop a single missile, and even the full system envisaged for 10 or 20 years down the road (if they can ever get the technology to work) could never stop an all-out Russian or Chinese attack. It's always easy to saturate a missile defence system.

But the day might come when a BMD system could stop most of what was left after an American first strike wiped out most Russian or Chinese missiles, and that is the prize that fascinates American strategists.

It's probably a pipe dream, but meanwhile the money keeps flowing to needy aerospace companies, the technology is delightfully challenging, and American taxpayers have bought the story about "rogue states."

Why on earth wouldn't we keep going?

"A broad and systematic international effort [is needed] to help [weak and failing] states move from the category of the failing to the category of the succeeding."

Promoting Globalization Will Reduce the Threat Posed by Rogue States

Banning N. Garrett and Dennis M. Sherman

Strategies that promote globalization will help failing and rogue states prosper and therefore reduce the threat these nations pose, claim Banning N. Garrett and Dennis M. Sherman in the following viewpoint. Struggling nations promote instability and terrorism worldwide, they contend, so multilateral strategies, including aid and help building strong institutions, will help end the economic and political isolation that make these nations a threat. Garrett is director of Asia programs at The Atlantic Council of the United States, and Sherman, a fellow at the council, is professor of business at the University of Wisconsin.

As you read, consider the following questions:

Banning N. Garrett and Dennis M. Sherman, "Non-Globalized States Pose a Threat," *Yale Global*, July 7, 2003. Reproduced by permission.

1. From where does the threat posed by weak and failing states emanate, according to Garrett and Sherman?

2. In the authors' opinion, when did the visibility of weak and failing states become more acute?

3. How have terrorists exacerbated the threats posed by failing states, in the authors' view?

The most immediate threats to the interests and security of the United States and other globalizing nations in the 21st century come not from each other or from rising powers but from declining states—weak, failing, and rogue nations that have become havens for terrorists and drug lords, seekers of weapons of mass destruction (WMD), incubators of disease, nurturers of religious extremists, and demographic time bombs of growing numbers of unemployed youth. President [George W.] Bush's [2003] visit to Africa can best be understood as part of a broader attempt to deal with the challenges emanating from these weak, failing and rogue states that have risen to the top of the U.S. national security agenda.

Failing to Participate in Globalization

While Globalization has created greater prosperity for states that have successfully integrated into the process, most states that have failed to effectively participate in globalization or have intentionally sought to isolate their countries from the process, have fallen farther behind. Weak and failing states are generally characterized by incomplete control over their national territories, an inability to provide basic services, a lack of legitimacy in the eyes of their populations, and widespread corruption and criminal violence. These states also usually have deteriorating infrastructures and weak, tenuous links to globalization.

The threats posed by the weak and failing states to the international community and their own populations emanate from the weaknesses of their governments. By contrast, the

Securing Peace Through Free Trade

The [2002] "National Security Strategy of the United States of America" says free trade and open markets can be as important to securing the peace for the long run as robust military funding.

The document represents new thinking in the government that U.S. security depends on economic success in other countries, that economic and political repression breed poverty, frustration and resentment, and that open markets—as well as open governments and open societies—can alleviate the causes of the terrorist threat against the West.

Gerald P. O'Driscoll and Sara J. Fitzgerald,
Orange County (Calif.) Register, *February 11, 2003.*

threats posed by rogue states, which also may have failing economies and impoverished populations and may be disconnected from globalization, emanate from the strengths of their governments. Rogue states threaten the international community through the acquisition of WMD and pursuit of aggressive military actions against their neighbors and even subnational groups within their own territories. Moreover, for rogue nations, WMD may be the balance of power equalizer of choice as they fall farther and farther behind economically and feel threatened by their neighbors or by the United States.

Weak and failing states have been present at least since post–World War II de-colonization, but the salience of the threats posed by these states has increased dramatically with the technological innovations and developments spurred by globalization and finally realized so devastatingly by the September 11th [2001] terrorist attacks on the US. The visibility of weak and failing states and the threats they pose had become more acute with the failure of communist and socialist policies worldwide, the demise of the Soviet Union and the end of two world economies (the U.S.-led capitalist economy versus the Soviet-led communist-bloc economy), which resulted in the acceleration of globalization. The end of the Cold War superpower competition in the Third World also led to the termination of U.S. and Soviet subsidies for Third World client regimes, which, in many ways, disguised these regimes' failure to build viable governments and economies.

The Empowerment of Terrorists

The threats posed by failing states have been exacerbated by the unparalleled empowerment of small groups of non-state actors, including terrorists, who have access to modern technologies, including both highly destructive weapons and communications and information systems. This empowerment of individuals and small groups has combined with the inability of failing states to control such groups operating and recruiting disaffected elements to terrorist causes within their borders. Ease of travel and communication in the closely integrated world enables terrorist groups to increasingly act globally. The United States and other major powers are now vulnerable to attacks planned and executed from bases thousands of miles away from the terrorists' homeland as was the case with Al Qaeda's September 11 operations from Afghanistan.

All of these trends have led to a new fuzzy bipolarity between the world of order, prosperity, relative stability and increasing interdependence and the world of growing disorder, economic decline, and instability. The latter consist of weak, failing and rogue nations that are far less connected with and benefiting far less—if at all—from the globalization process.

Despite the Bush administration's more aggressive stance and its unilateral use of force in dealing with threats from such states on the margin, the United States and all other participating states in globalization, face a strategic straightjacket that almost obligates them to cooperate rather than use force against each other. The Bush Administration's National Security Strategy (NSS) tacitly acknowledges this strategic shift. The NSS asserts that the threat to the United States and the world community does not emanate from the prospect of conflict among the world's great powers, which now compete in peace instead of continually preparing for war. Rather, the great powers find themselves on the same side, united by the common damages of terrorist violence and chaos as well as WMD proliferation that emanate from failing and rogue states.

Looking for International Cooperation

Although the Bush administration has called for global cooperation to meet these threats, international support for its actions and policies has been severely weakened by perceptions of U.S. arrogance and unilateralism and growing anti-Americanism. Indeed, the Bush administration's perceived unilateralism and more aggressive military posture has led the elites of many countries, including some U.S. allies, to desire to counterbalance and contain U.S. power while promoting multipolarity rather than to focus on common threats.

Meeting the threats and challenges of weak and failing states requires not only international cooperation in counterterrorism and non-proliferation, but a broad and systematic international effort to help these states move from the category of the failing to the category of the succeeding. Moreover, as former British Foreign Secretary Jack Straw warned in September 2002, state failure can no longer be seen as a localized or regional issue to be managed simply on an ad hoc, case by case basis. We have to develop a more coherent and effective international response which utilizes all of the tools at our disposal, ranging from aid and humanitarian assistance to support for institution building. In addition, Straw asserted, we need courage and foresight to bring our influence to bear at the point when a state begins to display the symptoms of failure, rather than when it is a lost cause.

> *"In a world where ... a gap exists between the richest and poorest peoples on earth [due to globalization], conflict is a natural outcome."*

Globalization Threatens Global Security

Arthur L. Dunklin

In the following viewpoint Arthur L. Dunklin argues that globalization has created a global income gap that breeds terrorism. The United States, which promotes and dominates the global free market, controls considerably more wealth than do the poorest nations, he maintains. This gap creates the resentments that motivate terrorist attacks, Dunklin claims. Rich countries must therefore narrow this gap, he asserts. Dunklin is a business professor at Columbia College and Kaplan University and senior diversity specialist at Western Washington University in Bellingham.

As you read, consider the following questions:

1. What statistics does Dunklin cite to support his assertion that globalization promotes inequality?

Arthur L. Dunklin, "Globalization: A Portrait of Exploitation, Inequality, and Limits," globalization.icaap.org, February 13, 2006. Reproduced by permission of the author.

2. According to the author, what image does the unfolding response to worldwide terror create?

3. In the author's opinion, how is globalization being challenged around the world?

Proponents argue that globalization has provided life-saving opportunities for millions of people around the world. They often point to increased trade, new and better technologies, expanded media, and economic growth as the tangible benefits of participating in a globalized economy. The dominant capitalist global marketplace (as the argument goes) has motivated some of the greatest innovations in world history, has led to the eradication of diseases, and has created wealth that far exceeds anything the world has ever known. Moreover, largely because of the social and technological advances made due to globalization, many people live longer and have higher standards of living.

The Harbinger of Inequality

If this is all true, then why is it, then, that so many people around the world harbor such an intense dislike and even hatred for that country which they see as the face of the new global marketplace—the United States of America? The answer to this question can be discerned—at least in part—in the amount of inequality that has resulted from globalization, with the United States as its principal proponent. I argue that these inequalities are a necessary component of US-conceived globalization.

While the benefits of globalization are significant and many lives are better off because of it, the global capitalist society is wrought with inequalities. The United States—consisting of four percent of the world's population—dominates all aspects of global free markets. Furthermore, the richest one percent of the world's population controls as much wealth as the poorest fifty-seven percent. As the United States experienced rapid economic growth over the past two decades, many poor countries, including some that were already counted among the world's poorest, experienced declining living standards. Per capita private consumption within the United States increased by 1.9 percent per year from 1980 to 1998, while during the same period, sub-Saharan Africa experienced a 1.2 percent annual decline. The expansion of the global marketplace has left half the world's population living on less than two dollars a day, and more than a billion people are currently living on less than one dollar a day. . . .

The Reach of Global Terror

The terrorist attacks of September 11, 2001 reminded many—while informing others—that not only is the world smaller in terms of communication flows and the export and import of goods and services, but it is also smaller in terms of the reach of global terror. No longer can vast oceans to the east and west and militarily benign neighbors to the north and south isolate a country from the reach of international terrorist organizations. Moreover, the currently unfolding response to worldwide terror provides an equally compelling portrayal of a world with universal problems that must be addressed through global means. Even the most economically and militarily powerful country on earth cannot defeat this threat by force. By breeding and supporting terrorist groups, countries residing in the periphery of the global economic order will force those countries that have benefited most from globalization to reduce the gap between the richest and poorest countries on earth.

The current approach to this threat is to seek out and arrest or kill terrorists while attempting to deny them the funding required for the execution of mass murder. However, the terrorist attacks on the United States also showed how these massive attacks can be executed without the need for significant monetary resources. Moreover, hostility to the institutions of globalization is being demonstrated by young and old in those countries that are exploited. Thus, the discontentment with globalization may be replenishing the terrorist pool even as the US and its allies seek to arrest or kill those who currently operate.

Conflicting Perceptions of America

As they begin to recognize the impact the disparity between rich and poor nations is having on their ability to live in peace, richer nations—the US in particular—have engaged in a campaign to present themselves as having compassion for the poor and disadvantaged of the world. From pledges to increase funding for AIDS vaccines to contributions to tsunami victims in Asia, the United States seeks to replace the image of a greedy, selfish nation with that of a compassionate one. However, the structural mechanisms that perpetuate inequality remain firmly in place. Moreover, the US continues to spend only a small percentage of its GNP [gross national product] on foreign aid to those countries most in need, and the entire continent of Africa remains largely ignored. The implications of such large disparities in living standards are significant and are likely to lead to increased resistance to global capitalism. Additionally, attacks on symbols of power are likely to increase just as they did in the decades following the great expansion of trade and investment in the last decades of the nineteenth century.

In a world where such a gap exists between the richest and poorest peoples on earth, conflict is a natural outcome. The concentration of military strength in the hands of the dominant power has historically maintained relative stability. However, in an age where an aircraft can be taken and used as a weapon for massive destruction against the most powerful nation on earth, military strength alone will no longer maintain stability. The current approach to world terror neglects to consider the systemic problems caused by global inequality.

A Worldwide Economic Apartheid

The world economy is going deeply wrong. The globalized free market results in patchy economic growth but is failing to deliver economic justice. A worldwide economic apartheid is developing in which around a billion people are doing exceptionally well; close to three billion are in poverty; and the rest are struggling as best they can.

Basic education, literacy and communications have meanwhile improved, people are far more aware of their position on the margins, and the end results already include social unrest, insurgencies and migratory pressures. Yet these are early days, and as the divisions widen, far greater instability is likely.

Paul Rogers, Manchester (UK) Guardian, *June 14, 2001.*

Although, some of those who carry out these acts do so out of religious fundamentalism, many hate the West—and the U.S. in particular—due to the policies advocated by core states that have created and perpetuated significant inequalities. Many see the US as controlling the global economy, either directly or through puppet organizations such as the IMF [International Monetary Fund] or the World Bank.

Voicing Opposition

While the US cannot maintain its hegemonic status forever, and states will continue to shift between the core and semi-periphery, a more equal distribution of wealth will not occur on its own. In the current age of advanced technologies where images of American wealth are beamed across the globe, conflict is a natural outcome of such dramatic inequalities. Unless capitalism is managed in a way that takes more consideration for weaker states, extreme poverty will likely continue to exist. This will benefit no one and core states have much to lose.

Today, globalization is being challenged around the world. Meetings of the institutions of globalization—the World Bank and the IMF—are met with intense violence and outrage. Those who see globalization as a force that has brought poverty to large parts of the world will continue to oppose it unless something is done to narrow the gap between the rich and the poor. If ideology continues to take precedence over pragmatism, conflict is an inevitable outcome. Just as other market-dominant minorities in history, the United States and other core states will always provoke intense resentments. The age of terrorism has brought with it the possibility that richer countries will be awakened to the plight of those countries that live in the periphery observing the displays of wealth exhibited by the rich nations operating in the core of the world system. No longer is narrowing the gap between rich and poor countries merely the humane and benevolent thing to do; it has become a matter of self-preservation for the rich countries.

A Need for New Policies

The current form of foreign aid the US provides to poorer countries is not only inadequate in amount, it is also inadequate in form. The use of dollars, medical aid, and food supplies ensures these poor countries will remain at the mercy of rich Western nations—the US in particular—and global institutions such as the World Bank and the IMF. The ability to effect real and lasting change is rooted in the development and proliferation of new technologies. Thus, if the rich nations of the West truly desire to close the economic gap between rich and poor nations, they must help poor countries develop the technologies that are more likely to lead to real change.

Moreover, the current design of the global marketplace favors the stronger markets of the West and of those countries that are allied with the United States. Even with its strong overall economic position, the US continues to protect the weaker segments of its economy from pure competition. To narrow the gap between the richest states and those that are unable to provide basic sustenance for their masses, the US should advocate for economic policies that are friendlier to poor states. Similar measures have been used throughout history. However, those efforts primarily targeted those states in which the US recognized a strategic military or economic interest.

A Nation's Values

Additionally, many of the poorest countries in the world are governed by rogue regimes that hoard large amounts of wealth while the majority of the population lives in poverty. Many of these regimes have been supported by the US to further its own interests. . . . The US articulates a love for freedom and human rights while supporting monarchs and dictators when it is necessary to further its own interests. A nation's values are more accurately depicted by what it does than by what it says. Accordingly, other nations view America's values through its actions. Too often, what they see is a rich and greedy nation that is only concerned about its own self-interests.

Few, if any, countries remain unaffected by globalization. While some countries have reaped the benefit of wealth the likes of which the world has never seen, others have grown poorer. Globalization has created an economically polarized world that is unsustainable over the long term. While protests from poor countries are not new, those protests have been largely ignored by countries with the wherewithal to create change. Inequality has not only been accepted as a byproduct of the current form of globalization, it has served as a necessary component of the global order. However, the gulf that exists today between the richest nations and the poorest ones has begun to reveal the limits of the exploitative capacity of globalization. Moreover, these limits are largely imposed by states residing in the periphery. Self-preservation dictates that wealthier nations narrow the economic gap between the rich and the poor.

Periodical Bibliography

The following articles have been selected to supplement the diverse views presented in this chapter.

American Legion	"The Threat of Weakness," December 2005.
Mona Charen	"How Not to Deal with a Threat," *Townhall.com*, July 29, 2005. www.townhall.com.
James H. Hughes	"The Ballistic Missile Threat: Defense and Technology," *Journal of Social, Political and Economic Studies*, Spring 2001.
Michael Kraig	"Gulf Security in a Globalizing World: Going Beyond US Hegemony," *YaleGlobal Online*, June 29, 2004. www.yaleglobal.yale.edu.
Anatol Lieven	"If You Can't Lick 'Em, Try Diplomacy," *International Herald Tribune*, September 10, 2005.
Tom Moriarty	"Entering the Valley of Uncertainty," *World Affairs*, Fall 2004.
Thomas M. Nichols	"Anarchy and Order in the New Age of Prevention," *World Policy Journal*, Fall 2005.
Ronald E. Powaski	"Many Sticks, Few Carrots," *America*, July 4–11, 2005.
Christopher Preble	"The Bush Doctrine and 'Rogue States,'" *Foreign Service Journal*, October 2005.
Jeffrey Record	"Nuclear Deterrence, Preventive War, and Counterproliferation," *Cato Policy Analysis*, July 8, 2004.
Ian Roxborough	"Taming the Hydra," *Dissent*, Fall 2005.
Leonard Weiss	"A High-Stakes Nuclear Gamble," *Los Angeles Times*, December 30, 2005.

For Further Discussion

Chapter 1

1. Ilan Berman contends that Iran's leadership and its pursuit of nuclear weapons pose a serious threat to global security. Dariush Zahedi and Omid Memarian claim, however, that Iran has serious internal weaknesses that threaten Iran's leadership and its nuclear weapons program. Examine the authors' affiliations. Does this influence which viewpoint you find more persuasive? Explain your reasoning.

2. Bruce Bennett and Carlton Meyer agree that North Korea's military is outdated and its economy is weak. Bennett believes these conditions make North Korea a serious threat while Meyer claims that such conditions make North Korea a feeble threat. What evidence does each author use to support his claim? Which evidence do you find more persuasive? Citing from their viewpoints, explain.

3. The authors in this chapter identify several nations that they believe to be serious rogue threats. Which nation do you believe poses the most serious threat to global security? Explain your answer, citing from the viewpoints.

Chapter 2

1. John R. Bolton contends that rogue nations are defying the Non-Proliferation Treaty to pursue nuclear weapons. Mario Basini argues that such claims against rogue nations are hypocritical because the United States continues to maintain a vast nuclear arsenal. Both authors agree, however, that rogue nations with nuclear weapons pose a serious threat. Which author's strategy would be more effective in your opinion? Why?

2. Yoram Schweitzer contends that rogue nations actively support terrorism to achieve state goals. Benjamin R. Barber contends, on the other hand, that terrorists merely use states to achieve their own independent goals. Based on the viewpoints in this and other chapters in this anthology, which states do you believe actively sponsor terrorists to achieve state goals and which states do terrorists use to achieve their own goals? Explain your reasoning, citing from the viewpoints.

3. The authors in this chapter point to several threats posed by rogue nations. Which threat do you believe is the most serious and which rogue nation do you believe is the most serious offender? Explain your answer.

Chapter 3

1. Kay Seok, Sam Brownback, Human Rights Watch, and Vernon Coleman cite nations that they argue violate human rights. Other nations violate the same human rights as those identified by the authors in this chapter. Why are the nations in this chapter considered rogue nations while others are not? For which nations do you think the rogue label is justified? Are the human rights violations of any other nations egregious enough to warrant being on your list of rogues? Explain your answers, citing from the viewpoints in this and other chapters.

2. Do you agree with Joseph Loconte that oppressive regimes known for genocide or political and religious repression should not be allowed to serve on the UN Commission on Human Rights? If you agree, how should member nations be selected? What challenges will this commission face when trying to enforce human rights sanctions against nations it refuses membership? If you disagree, how can the commission ensure that its members do not ignore human rights violations within their own borders?

3. According to Phyllis Bennis, U.S. intervention does not spread democracy or improve human rights in the Middle East. What strategies does she recommend that would spread democracy and human rights in the Middle East? Do you agree, or do you think U.S. intervention is necessary? Explain, citing from the viewpoints in this chapter.

Chapter 4

1. The authors in this chapter debate several different strategies to contain or reduce the threat posed by rogue states. Which strategy do you believe would be most effective? Explain.

2. The editors of the *National Review* believe that the United States should use preemptive force against rogue nations it believes have developed weapons of mass destruction. Ivan Eland claims that this policy has backfired, increasing rogue nations' efforts to obtain such weapons. Which viewpoint do you find more persuasive? Why?

3. Dennis Ross and Gwynne Dyer disagree over the usefulness and feasibility of a missile defense system. What evidence does each cite to support his claim? Which evidence do you find more persuasive? Explain, citing evidence from the viewpoints.

4. Arthur L. Dunklin disagrees with Banning N. Garrett and Dennis M. Sherman's claim that globalization will reduce the threat posed by rogue nations. These authors also have opposing views on the economic impact of globalization. How do the authors view the economic impact of globalization? Are these views central to their claims about globalization's impact on rogue nations? Explain, citing from the viewpoints.

Organizations to Contact

American Enterprise Institute (AEI)
1150 Seventeenth St. NW, Washington, DC 20036
(202) 862-5800 • fax: (202) 862-7177
Web site: www.aei.org

AEI is a conservative think tank based in Washington, D.C. Its members support a strong and well-funded military and the use of force against rogue nations, particularly those that support terrorism. AEI publishes the magazine *American Enterprise*. Other publications include reports and papers such as "Fighting Terror: Lessons and Implications from the Iraqi Theater" and "Brave New World: An Enduring Pax Americana," which are available on its Web site.

American Foreign Policy Council (AFPC)
1521 Sixteenth St. NW, Washington, DC 20036
(202) 462-6055 • fax: (202) 462-6045
e-mail: afpc@afpc.org
Web site: www.afpc.org

Founded in 1982 AFPC is a nonprofit organization dedicated to bringing information to those who make or influence the foreign policy of the United States and to assisting world leaders with building democracies and market economies. AFPC publishes bulletins on foreign policy issues, including the *Missile Defense Briefing Report*. On its Web site AFPC publishes links to articles concerning U.S. policy toward rogue nations, including "The Diplomatic Dance Won't Do" and "Averting a Nuclear Nightmare."

The Brookings Institution
1775 Massachusetts Ave. NW, Washington, DC 20036
(202) 797-6000 • fax: (202) 797-6004
e-mail: brookinfo@brook.edu
Web site: www.brook.edu

Founded in 1927, the institution conducts research and analyzes global events and their impact on the United States and on U.S. foreign policy. It publishes the *Brookings Review* quarterly as well as numerous books and research papers on foreign policy. Numerous reports on foreign policy and rogue nations are available on the institution's Web site, including "The New National Security Strategy and Preemption" and "A 'Master' Plan to Deal with North Korea."

Cato Institute
1000 Massachusetts Ave. NW, Washington, DC 20001-5403
(202) 842-0200 • fax: (202) 842-3490
Web site: www.cato.org

The institute is a libertarian public policy research foundation dedicated to peace and limited government intervention in foreign affairs. It publishes numerous reports and periodicals, including *Policy Analysis* and *Cato Policy Review*, both of which discuss U.S. policy in regional conflicts. Cato members also publish analysis and commentary opposing the U.S. invasion of Iraq and the use of force against other nations thought to support terrorism.

Center for Strategic and International Studies (CSIS)
1800 K St. NW, Washington, DC 20006
(202) 887-0200 • fax: (202) 775-3199
Web site: www.csis.org

CSIS is a public policy research institution that specializes in the analysis of U.S. domestic and foreign policy, national security, and economic policy. The center analyzes world crises and recommends U.S. military and defense policies. Its publications include the journal *The Washington Quarterly* and the reports "Change and Challenge on the Korean Peninsula: Developments, Trends, and Issues" and "Combating Chemical, Biological, Radiological, and Nuclear Terrorism: A Comprehensive Strategy."

Council on Foreign Relations (CFR)
58 E. Sixty-eighth St., New York, NY   10021
(212) 434-9400 • fax: (212) 986-2984
Web site: www.cfr.org

The council specializes in foreign affairs and studies the international aspects of American political and economic policies and problems. Its journal *Foreign Affairs*, published five times a year, includes analyses of current conflicts around the world. Articles and commentary by CFR members are available on its Web site, including the report "A New National Security Strategy in an Age of Terrorists, Tyrants, and Weapons of Mass Destruction."

Foreign Policy Association (FPA)
470 Park Ave. South, 2nd Floor., New York, NY   10016
(212) 481-8100 • fax: (212) 481-9275
e-mail: info@fpa.org
Web site: www.fpa.org

The FPA is a nonprofit organization that believes a concerned and informed public is the foundation for an effective foreign policy. Publications such as the annual *Great Decisions* briefing book and the quarterly offerings of the Headline Series review U.S. foreign policy issues in China, the Middle East, and Africa. The FPA's Global Q & A series offers interviews with leading U.S. and foreign officials on issues concerning the Middle East, intelligence gathering, weapons of mass destruction, and military and diplomatic initiatives.

Global Exchange
2017 Mission St., #303, San Francisco, CA   94110
(415) 255-7296 • fax: (415) 255-7498
Web site: www.globalexchange.org

Global Exchange is a human rights organization that exposes economic and political injustices around the world. As responses to such injustices, the organization supports education, activism, and a noninterventionist U.S. foreign policy.

Global Exchange believes that the terrorist attacks of September 11, 2001, do not justify U.S. retaliation against civilian populations. It opposed the U.S. invasions of Afghanistan and Iraq and supports an end to the trade embargo against Cuba. The organization publishes *Global Exchanges* quarterly.

The Heritage Foundation
214 Massachusetts Ave. NE, Washington, DC   20002-4999
(800) 544-4843 • fax: (202) 544-6979
e-mail: pubs@heritage.org
Web site: www.heritage.org

The foundation is a conservative public policy research institute that advocates limited government and the free-market system. The foundation publishes the quarterly *Insider* as well as monographs, books, and papers supporting U.S. noninterventionism. Heritage publications on U.S. foreign policy include "Why U.S. Troops Should Not Be Sent to Liberia," "Iran: Revolting Against the Revolution?" and "Resolving the North Korean Nuclear Issue."

Resource Center for Nonviolence
515 Broadway, Santa Cruz, CA   95060
(831) 423-1626 • fax: (831) 423-8716
e-mail: rcnv@rcnv.org
Web site: www.rcnv.org

The Resource Center for Nonviolence was founded in 1976 and promotes nonviolence as a force for personal and social change. It opposed the war in Iraq and supports peace protests to help prevent future U.S. military actions. The center provides speakers, workshops, leadership development, and nonviolence training programs and publishes a newsletter, *Center Report*, twice a year.

United Nations Association of the United States of America
801 Second Ave., New York, NY   10017
(212) 907-1300
Web site: www.unausa.org

The association is a nonpartisan, nonprofit research organization dedicated to strengthening both the United Nations and U.S. participation in the UN Security Council. Its publications include the bimonthly newspaper the *Interdependent* and the reports "Rebuilding Iraq: How the United States and United Nations Can Work Together," and "The Use of Force, Legitimacy, and the U.N. Charter."

U.S. Department of State
2201 C St. NW, Washington, DC   20520
Web site: www.state.gov

The State Department is a federal agency that advises the president on the formulation and execution of foreign policy. The department's Office of Counterterrorism publishes the annual report "Patterns of Global Terrorism," which lists the nations that the United States has designated as state sponsors of terrorism; a list of most wanted terrorists; and pages providing background information on every country in the world.

Bibliography of Books

T.D. Allman — *Rogue State: America at War with the World.* New York: Nation Books, 2004.

Andrew J. Bacevich — *American Empire: The Realities and Consequences of U.S. Diplomacy.* Cambridge, MA: Harvard University Press, 2002.

Jasper Becker — *Rogue State: The Continuing Threat of North Korea.* New York: Oxford University Press, 2005.

William Blum — *Rogue State: A Guide to the World's Only Superpower.* Monroe, ME: Common Courage Press, 2005.

Max Boot — *The Savage Wars of Peace: Small Wars and the Rise of American Power.* New York, Basic Books, 2002.

Peter Brookes — *A Devil's Triangle: Terrorism, Weapons of Mass Destruction, and Rogue States.* Lanham, MD: Rowman & Littlefield, 2005.

Zbigniew Brzezinski — *Choice: Domination or Leadership.* New York, Basic Books, 2004.

Fraser Cameron — *U.S. Foreign Policy After the Cold War: Global Hegemon or Reluctant Sheriff?* New York: Routledge, 2002.

Noam Chomsky — *Rogue States: The Rule of Force in World Affairs.* London: Pluto, 2000.

Ivan Eland — *The Empire Has No Clothes: U.S. Foreign Policy Exposed.* Oakland, CA: Independent Institute, 2004.

Ivan Eland — *Putting "Defense" Back into U.S. Defense Policy.* Westport, CT: Praeger, 2001.

Jim Garrison — *America as Empire: Global Leader or Rogue Power?* San Francisco: Berrett-Koehler, 2004.

Jack L. Goldsmith and Eric A. Posner — *Do International Norms Influence State Behavior?* New York: Oxford University Press, 2005.

Gabriel Kolko — *Another Century of War?* New York: New Press, 2002.

Paul Krugman — *The Great Unraveling: Losing Our Way in the New Century.* New York, Norton, 2003.

Charles A. Kupchan — *The End of the American Era: U.S. Foreign Policy and the Geopolitics of the Twenty-First Century.* New York: Vintage, 2003.

Jan Lodal — *The Price of Dominance: The New Weapons of Mass Destruction and Their Challenge to American Leadership.* New York: Council on Foreign Relations, 2001.

Walter Russell Mead — *Power, Terror, Peace and War: America's Grand Strategy in a World at Risk.* New York: Knopf, 2004.

Michael E. O'Hanlon — *Defense Policy Choices for the Bush Administration*. Washington, DC: Brookings Institution, 2001.

Robert M. Perito — *Where Is the Lone Ranger When We Need Him? America's Search for a Postconflict Stability Force*. Washington, DC: United States Institute for Peace, 2004.

Clyde V. Prestowitz — *Rogue Nation: American Unilateralism and the Failure of Good Intentions*. New York: Basic Books, 2003.

George Soros — *The Bubble of American Supremacy: Correcting the Misuse of American Power*. New York: Public Affairs, 2003.

Joseph E. Stiglitz — *Globalization and Its Discontents*. New York: Norton, 2002.

William C. Triplett — *Rogue State: How a Nuclear North Korea Threatens America*. Washington, DC: Regnery, 2004.

William Walker — *Weapons of Mass Destruction and International Order*. New York: Oxford University Press, 2004.

Index